Exercising Essential Statistics

Third Edition

Evan M. Berman Ph.D.

XiaoHu Wang Ph.D.

 |
SAGE   CQPRESS

Los Angeles | London | New Delhi
Singapore | Washington DC

CQPRESS

Los Angeles | London | New Delhi
Singapore | Washington DC

FOR INFORMATION:

CQ Press
An Imprint of SAGE Publications, Inc.
2455 Teller Road
Thousand Oaks, California 91320
E-mail: order@sagepub.com

SAGE Publications Ltd.
1 Oliver's Yard
55 City Road
London, EC1Y 1SP
United Kingdom

SAGE Publications India Pvt. Ltd.
B 1/I 1 Mohan Cooperative Industrial Area
Mathura Road, New Delhi 110 044
India

SAGE Publications Asia-Pacific Pte. Ltd.
33 Pekin Street #02-01
Far East Square
Singapore 048763

Acquisitions Editor: Charisse Kiino
Production Editor: Elizabeth Kline
Copy Editor: Amy Marks
Typesetter: C&M Digitals, (P) Ltd.
Proofreader: Stefanie Storholt
Cover Designer: Vincent Hughes
Marketing Manager: Christopher O'Brien

Printed in the United States of America

ISBN-13: 978-1-60871-676-0

This book is printed on acid-free paper.

11 12 13 14 15 10 9 8 7 6 5 4 3 2 1

CONTENTS

Chapter 6　Central Tendency

Chapter 7　Measures of Dispersion

Chapter 8　Contingency Tables

Chapter 9　Getting Results

Chapter 10　Hypothesis Testing with Chi-Square

Chapter 11　Measures of Association

Chapter 12　The T-Test

Chapter 13　Analysis of Variance (ANOVA)

INTRODUCTION

This workbook is an integral part of the *Essential Statistics for Public Managers and Policy Analysts,* Third Edition, package. Whereas the textbook introduces concepts and offers examples of statistical applications, the workbook further strengthens understanding by illustrating applications and encouraging analysts to think through statistical concepts in new and engaging ways. In short, the applications found here are key to mastering statistics.

Chapters 1 through 18 correspond to those in the textbook. The "Chapter Objectives" at the beginning of each textbook chapter are a good guide to what you will be practicing in each workbook chapter. To help students understand new concepts, four different sections are featured that target different aspects of learning. Specifically, each of these chapters is divided into the following sections:

- "Q & A" facilitates student learning of the statistical concepts through questions and answers. It is an ideal study guide for tests.
- "Critical Thinking" comprises short exercises to stimulate further conceptual insights into statistics and applications.
- "Application Exercises" in Chapters 1–5 or "Data-Based Exercises" in Chapters 6–18 help students develop hands-on skills using practical applications. The exercises in Chapters 6–18 draw on datasets provided on the accompanying CD.
- "Further Reading" lists work toward self-study in areas of interest to readers, including articles that students may wish to access.

This workbook also includes chapters that extend the material covered in the textbook. Chapter 19 is new to this third edition and is a user's guide to essential statistics in Excel. Chapter 20 describes how to use SPSS, a statistical analysis program. It provides a step-by-step approach for ease of learning. Chapter 21 provides documentation for the datasets provided on the accompanying CD. The datasets are provided in SPSS, SAS, SYSTAT, and Stata formats for easy use.

The enclosed CD also provides bonus data and a complete report based on an actual citizen survey. The report and survey instrument are available electronically in Microsoft Word for your convenience. In addition, the CD includes a presentation in Microsoft PowerPoint, which will help users stretch their imaginations as they think about how to present their data to others in the public realm. A file discussing the use of spreadsheets in public management and analysis, including examples in Microsoft Excel, is also included on the CD.

We hope that this workbook will help users in their learning. Moreover, we hope they are able to readily apply some of these exercises to problems in their workplaces.

Have a question or feedback? Just send us an e-mail, and we'll be happy to respond. Let us know what works for you and how we can further improve this workbook. We look forward to hearing from you.

Evan M. Berman
evanmberman@gmail.com

XiaoHu Wang
xwang1989@gmail.com

CHAPTER

1

Why Statistics for Public Managers and Analysts?

Q & A

1. Identify five ways in which analysis and data often are used.

The five ways are as follows: (1) to describe and analyze societal problems, (2) to describe policies and programs, (3) to monitor progress and prevent fraud, (4) to improve program operations, and (5) to evaluate policy and program outcomes.

2. How does quantitative analysis assist in decision making?

Quantitative analysis provides a factual underpinning of situations and responses by quantifying the extent of problems and situations and the actual or likely impact of proposed strategies. At the very least, a focus on facts and objective analysis can reduce judgment errors stemming from overly impressionistic or subjective perceptions that are factually incorrect.

3. Identify six competencies for analysis.

The six competencies are (1) being familiar with data sources in your line of work, (2) being able to collect your own data, (3) analyzing data, (4) communicating results from analysis, (5) bringing to quantitative analysis the theory and practice of management and policy analysis, and (6) having a strong sense of ethics relating to quantitative analysis.

4. What is scientific research?

Scientific research is the careful, systematic process of inquiry that leads to the discovery or interpretation of facts, behaviors, and theories. Scientific research is distinguished from personal and other forms of research or inquiry by rather strict standards for accepting new facts and theories as knowledge and by a process that includes other scientists in making such determinations.

5. What is statistics?

Statistics is the body of systematic knowledge and practice that provides standards and procedures for drawing conclusions from one's data. Statistics includes specific tools for analyzing data, too.

6. Identify four stages of proficiency in quantitative analysis.

The four stages of proficiency are: know nothing, journeyman, technocrat, and sophisticated expert. Each stage is associated with distinct development objectives.

7. What three areas of ethical concern are identified in connection with analysis?

The three areas are as follows: (1) fully disclosing the purposes of analysis, (2) integrity in analysis and communication, and (3) concern for the impact of analysis and research on the welfare of human subjects.

8. *What is scientific misconduct?*

Scientific misconduct is generally understood as the violation of the standard norms of scholarly conduct and ethical behavior in scientific research. Scientific misconduct, when considered by others to be significant or severe, can diminish one's reputation and negatively affect one's career, including the possibility of dismissal from one's job and adverse legal action.

9. *What is the specific problem of dual purposes?*

Analysts must balance potentially conflicting purposes of (1) furthering programs and policies and (2) establishing objective truths about how well a program is performing.

10. *Which practices are associated with furthering the integrity of analysis and communication?*

Analysts should be honest, objective, accurate, and complete. Analysts should not hide facts, change data, falsify results, or consider only data that support a favored conclusion. Analysts should also fully report the sources of their data, data collection methodologies, and any possible gaps and shortfalls, and they should assess the impact of such shortcomings on their findings. Results should be presented in straightforward and nonmisleading ways. These norms provide essential guidance to analysts throughout the entire analytical process.

11. *What concern should analysts have for the impact of research on the welfare of human subjects?*

Researchers and analysts should recognize and minimize the potential harm that their research and analysis could have on research subjects. Most human subjects research is now subject to oversight by institutional review boards to ensure that risks to subjects are reasonable and that possible harm is identified and minimized.

CRITICAL THINKING

Note to students: These questions further understanding of selected, key points made in the textbook. Questions in the next section, "Application Exercises," are designed to encourage application of the key points in practice.

1. **What is the difference between describing the extent of a social problem and describing the factors that give rise to it? Give an example. How can the latter be useful for developing programs and policies?**

   _____
   _____
   _____
   _____
   _____
   _____

2. **What is the role of statistics in connection with the six competencies mentioned in the text? What else might be needed to attain these competencies?**

   _____
   _____
   _____
   _____
   _____
   _____

3. Many programs produce routine, administrative data that are used to monitor progress and prevent fraud. How useful are such data for the five common uses of analysis and data mentioned in the text? What other data might be needed, such as might be obtained from citizen or client surveys?

_____

_____

_____

_____

_____

_____

4. Identify a person or situation associated with each of the four stages of proficiency in quantitative analysis.

_____

_____

_____

_____

_____

_____

5. Explain how the following concerns of ethics can affect research and its utilization: (1) dual purposes, (2) full disclosure, (3) truthfulness, (4) alternative explanations, (5) communication, and (6) well-being of human subjects. Give examples of each.

_____

_____

_____

_____

_____

_____

APPLICATION EXERCISES

Note to students: This section is called "Data-Based Exercises" in later chapters (starting in Chapter 6) and will provide you with hands-on exercises that involve real datasets.

1. Identify five problems or challenges in your area of interest that would benefit from analysis or research.

_____

_____

_____

_____

_____

2. Identify at least two examples, in your area of interest, of each of the five common uses of analysis and data.

_____

_____

_____

_____

_____

3. What data exist in your area of interest? Are there any datasets with which managers and analysts are expected to be familiar?

_____

_____

_____

_____

_____

4. At what stage of proficiency do you see yourself? What is necessary to get beyond this stage? Develop some learning objectives for yourself.

_____

_____

_____

_____

_____

5. Explain how a customer or citizen survey might be useful in your area of interest. What topics might such a survey address? What challenges do you foresee?

_____

_____

_____

_____

_____

6. (a) Consider the following proposition: "Almost every department needs people with analytical skills." Verify this proposition by interviewing managers in your area of interest. Which analytical skills do they say that they are looking for? (b) Also, research salaries at the U.S. Bureau of Labor, National Industry-Specific Occupational Employment and Wage Estimates, at www.bls.gov/oes/current/oessrci.htm, and compare wages for occupations that vary in analytical content, for example, management positions in budgeting, information technology, human resource management, and parks and recreation.

_____

_____

_____

_____

_____

7. Identify and consider some ethical situations that would challenge the integrity of your analysis and research, such as being asked to withhold relevant information. How might you deal with such situations?

_____

_____

_____

_____

_____

8. **Research the policies and practices that pertain to ethics in research in your agency or in an agency in your area of interest. If there are none, suggest two or three that would serve as a foundation for a more extensive set of policies.**

_____

_____

_____

_____

_____

FURTHER READING

Various books offer additional information about the importance and uses of research and analysis in public service. A classic text about the use of analysis is Aaron Wildavski, *Speaking Truth to Power: The Art and Craft of Policy Analysis* (Piscataway, N.J.: Transaction Publishers, 1987). Books on policy analysis support the need for research methods and data analysis, such as Eugene Bardach, *Practical Guide for Policy Analysis: The Eightfold Path to More Effective Problem Solving*, 4th ed. (Washington, D.C.: CQ Press, 2011) or William Dunn, *Public Policy Analysis: An Introduction* (New York: Prentice Hall, 2009). Scholarship about the use of policy analysis and research in this area traces back to the development of policy analysis as a field in the 1970s and efforts to get public agencies to use it in the 1970s and 1980s. Since then, research has focused varyingly on the capacity of government organizations to develop or have policy research and analysis capabilities, and the utilization of such knowledge in their decision-making processes.

Different events and contexts lead to different foci in research. In recent years, a focus has been the utilization of "evidenced-based" policy, resulting from increased capacity of performance measurement (see Chapter 4) and policy analysis. A representative article in this genre is M. Howlett, "Policy Analytical Capacity and Evidence-Based Policy-Making: Lessons from Canada," *Canadian Public Administration* 52 (2009): 153–175. As this source suggests, the problem of research utilization is found throughout the world. Another article is R. Landry, M. Lamari, and N. Amara, "The Extent and Determinants of the Utilization of University Research in Government Agencies," *Public Administration Review* 63 (March/April 2003): 192–205. This article received the Louis Brownlow Award from the American Society for Public Administration for the best article published in *Public Administration Review* in 2003. Earlier, the focus was on the development of performance measurement. See, for example, E. Berman and X. Wang, "Performance Measurement in U.S. Counties: Capacity for Reform," *Public Administration Review* 60 (September/October 2000): 409–420, which reflects the then-growing development of performance measures in local government. But as times change, so, too, does research.

A classic book about the ethics of analysis is Darrell Huff, *How to Lie with Statistics* (New York: Norton, 1993). Another book on this topic is Joel Best, *More Damned Lies and Statistics: How Numbers Confuse Public Issues* (Berkeley: University of California Press, 2004). The National Institutes of Health website provides educational materials that discuss protections for human subjects, which is applicable to all types of research, including studies that public policy managers and analysts might conduct that involve humans in some way, for example, by administering surveys. Training materials related to approval processes for such research (such as by institutional review board that are found at many research centers and universities) may also be found on the web (see, for example, http://bioethics.od.nih.gov/IRB.html).

CHAPTER

2

Research Design

Note to students: This chapter includes questions and exercises relating to the textbook introduction to Section II (Research Methods), indicated by SI (Section Introduction).

Q & A

1. What is research methodology? (SI)

Research methodology is the science of methods for investigating phenomena. Research methods are used in almost every social science discipline and can be applied to many different kinds of problems, including those found in public and nonprofit management and analysis.

2. What is basic research? What is applied research? (SI)

Basic research is a research activity whose purpose is to develop new knowledge about phenomena such as problems, events, programs or policies, and their relationships. Applied research is a research activity whose purpose is to develop knowledge for addressing practical problems.

3. What are quantitative research methods? What are qualitative research methods? (SI)

Quantitative research methods involve the collection of data that can be analyzed using statistical methods. The purpose of quantitative research is to quantify the magnitude of phenomena, to provide statistical evidence about factors affecting these phenomena, and to quantify the impacts of programs and policies. Qualitative research methods involve the collection and analysis of words, symbols, or artifacts that are largely nonstatistical in nature. Typically the purpose of qualitative research is to identify and describe new phenomena and their relationships.

4. What are variables?

Variables are empirically observable phenomena that vary.

5. What are attributes?

Attributes are the specific characteristics of a variable, that is, the specific ways in which a variable can vary. All variables have attributes. For example, the variable "gender" has two attributes: male and female.

6. How is descriptive analysis different from the study of relationships?

Descriptive analysis provides information about (the level of) individual variables, whereas the study of relationships provides information about the relationships among variables.

7. Define the terms independent variable and dependent variable.

All causal relationships have independent and dependent variables. The dependent variable is the variable that is affected (caused) by one or more independent variables. Independent variables are variables that cause an effect on other variables but are not themselves shaped by other variables.

8. What is a causal relationship, and how is it different from an association?

Most studies describe relationships among variables. When relationships are causal, one variable is said to be the cause of another. When variables are only associated with each other, no effort is made to identify patterns of causation.

9. What is required for establishing a claim of causality?

To establish causality, there must be both empirical correlation and a plausible theory that explains how these variables are causally related.

10. What is a hypothesis?

A hypothesis is a relationship that has not yet been tested empirically.

11. What six steps are involved in program evaluation?

The six steps are as follows: (1) defining program goals and activities, (2) identifying which key relationships will be studied, (3) determining what type of research design will be used, (4) defining and measuring study concepts, (5) collecting and analyzing program data, and (6) presenting study findings.

12. What are rival hypotheses? What are control variables?

Rival hypotheses state threats to the credibility of study conclusions. Control variables are variables used in empirical research to evaluate rival hypotheses.

13. Explain the role of statistics in determining the impact of rival hypotheses (or control variables) on program outcomes.

The impact of rival hypotheses can seldom be ascertained through research design alone. Statistics, then, are used to examine these impacts. (Statistics are also used for other purposes, explained in subsequent chapters of *Essential Statistics for Public Managers and Policy Analysts.*)

14. How are quasi-experimental designs different from classic, randomized experiments?

In a classic experimental design, participants are randomly assigned to either a control or an experimental group. The *only* systematic difference between the groups is that study group participants receive an intervention (called a stimulus, such as a therapy, subsidy, or training). Any outcome differences between these two groups are then attributed to the systematic difference—the treatment. Such testing conditions are seldom possible in public management and policy. Quasi-experimental designs are imperfect research designs that may lack baselines, comparison groups, or randomization, which are present in classic, randomized experiments.

15. What are threats to external validity?

Threats to external validity are those that jeopardize the generalizability of study conclusions to other situations. These threats often concern unique features of the study population or research design.

16. What are threats to internal validity?

Threats to internal validity are those that jeopardize study conclusions about whether an intervention in fact caused a difference in the study population. These threats often question the logic of study conclusions.

CRITICAL THINKING

1. Give examples of basic and applied research questions that might be raised in the context of (1) a program to reduce adult illiteracy and (2) a program that fights international terrorism. (SI)

   _____
   _____
   _____
   _____
   _____
   _____

2. Why are both quantitative and qualitative methods indispensable in addressing questions of basic and applied research? (SI)

   _____
   _____
   _____
   _____
   _____
   _____

3. Give some examples of variables. Why are variables key to research?

   _____
   _____
   _____
   _____
   _____
   _____

4. A program aims to reduce adult illiteracy by providing reading sessions during evening hours. Identify the dependent and independent variables.

   _____
   _____
   _____
   _____
   _____
   _____

5. A study examines the impact of gender and drug use on school performance and political orientations. Identify the dependent and independent variables.

   _____
   _____
   _____
   _____
   _____
   _____

6. It is said that in Sweden an empirical association exists between the presence of storks and the incidence of new babies. Explain what is necessary to establish a claim of causation. Do storks really bring babies?

    _____

    _____

    _____

    _____

    _____

    _____

7. A study examines the relationship between race and crime. Is this a causal relationship or an association? Explain.

    _____

    _____

    _____

    _____

    _____

    _____

8. Apply the following statement to program evaluation: "Research begins with asking questions." Think about a program that you know about as a basis for answering this question.

    _____

    _____

    _____

    _____

    _____

    _____

9. The developers of the adult literacy program mentioned in question 4 claim that the program is effective. By what measures might this effectiveness be demonstrated?

    _____

    _____

    _____

    _____

    _____

    _____

10. What might be some rival hypotheses regarding the effectiveness of this adult literacy program?

    _____

    _____

    _____

    _____

    _____

    _____

11. Discuss an experimental research design for testing the effectiveness of an anger management program. Then apply the three quasi-experimental designs mentioned in Box 2.2 in the text.

_____
_____
_____
_____
_____
_____

APPLICATION EXERCISES

1. Give examples of basic and applied research questions in your area of interest. (SI)

_____
_____
_____
_____
_____

2. Give examples of quantitative and qualitative research methods in your area of interest. (SI)

_____
_____
_____
_____
_____

3. Consider the following variables: the number of immigrants, attitudes toward abortion, and environmental pollution. What might be some attributes of each of the variables?

_____
_____
_____
_____
_____

4. You have been asked to develop a neighborhood crime control program. Thinking ahead, you develop a strategy for evaluating the program in subsequent months and years. Define the program and identify dependent and independent variables that can be used to evaluate it.

_____
_____
_____
_____

5. Identify a problem in your area of interest. Identify the dependent and one or more independent variables affecting this problem.

    _____

    _____

    _____

    _____

    _____

6. Consider a program or policy in your area of interest. How do the specific issues raised in the text regarding program evaluation apply to your program or policy? For instance, give some examples of how difficult it can be to document program outcomes.

    _____

    _____

    _____

    _____

    _____

7. Discuss how you can apply the six steps of program evaluation to a specific program in your area of interest.

    _____

    _____

    _____

    _____

    _____

8. Find an article that discusses a specific program evaluation and identify in it each of the six steps of program evaluation.

    _____

    _____

    _____

    _____

    _____

9. Identify some rival hypotheses (control variables) that might affect conclusions about the effectiveness of an adult literacy program. Then, discuss how an experimental research design and several quasi-experimental designs might be helpful for determining the effectiveness of the program.

    _____

    _____

    _____

    _____

    _____

10. Define the objectives of a job training program, and then identify some rival hypotheses regarding possible outcomes. Explain how baselines and comparison groups might be used.

    _____

    _____

    _____

    _____

    _____

FURTHER READING

The all-time, best-selling, easy-to-read general textbook on **research methods** in social science (general) is Earl Babbie, *The Practice of Social Research,* 12th ed. or later (Belmont, Calif.: Wadsworth, 2009). A book with a focus on statistics in public administration is Kaifeng Yang and Gerald Miller, *Handbook of Research Methods in Public Administration,* 2nd ed. (New York: Marcel Dekker, 2008). A variety of books on **program evaluation** may be found readily online, and we encourage readers to choose one. An example is J. Fitzpatrick et al., *Program Evaluation: Alternative Approaches and Practical Guidelines,* 4th ed. (Upper Saddle River, N.J.: Prentice Hall, 2010). Another source with applications in public administration is Joseph Wholey et al., eds., *Handbook of Practical Program Evaluation,* 3rd ed. (San Francisco: Jossey Bass, 2010). A classic book on program evaluation is Peter Rossi et al., *Evaluation: A Systematic Approach,* 7th ed. or later (Thousand Oaks, Calif.: Sage, 2003), but that book is now getting dated.

Research methods are used widely in scholarly research, of course. The *Journal of Policy Analysis and Management* publishes many articles that evaluate specific programs and policies. Some of these articles are grounded in economic thought, though not all. Also, most empirical articles in the leading journals in public administration, political science, and nonprofit management use the terminology of independent, dependent, and control variables discussed in this chapter. You should have no problem picking up any leading, scholarly journal in your field and finding these terms used. A few studies in public and nonprofit management and policy analysis use comparison groups and quasi-experimental designs, but most rely on statistical techniques to account for control variables. These techniques are discussed later in the textbook.

Conceptualization and Measurement

Q & A

1. What is a scale?

A scale is the collection of attributes that is used to measure a specific variable. Scales are important because they define the nature of information about variables.

2. What is a nominal-level scale? What is an ordinal-level scale?

A nominal-level scale exhibits no ordering among the categories. The variable "region" is an example of a variable with a nominal scale. An ordinal-level scale exhibits order among categories, though without exact distances between successive categories. Likert scales are examples of ordinal scales. Variables with ordinal- or nominal-level scales are called categorical (or discrete) variables.

3. What is an interval-level scale? What is a ratio-level scale?

Interval- and ratio-level scales exhibit both order and distance among categories. The only difference between interval and ratio scales is that the latter have a true zero. Income is an example of a ratio-level variable when it is measured in actual dollars; someone who earns $75,000 per year makes exactly three times that of someone making $25,000, and it is possible to make $0 (no income). The distinction between ratio- and interval-level variables is typically of little relevance to public and nonprofit administration and policy analysis. Variables with interval- and ratio-level scales are also called continuous variables.

4. What are incomplete, ambiguous, and overlapping scales? Why must they be avoided?

An incomplete scale omits response categories, an ambiguous scale has ill-defined response categories, and an overlapping scale has at least one response that is covered by more than one category. Incomplete, ambiguous, and overlapping scales should be avoided because they have limited measurement validity.

5. Define and contrast the terms variable and concept.

Variables are empirically observable phenomena that vary, whereas concepts are abstract ideas. Variables are observed directly; concepts are observed indirectly (through variables).

6. Describe the two steps involved in concept measurement.

Concept measurement involves two steps: first, the process of specifying all relevant dimensions of concepts (conceptualization) and, second, the process of specifying which variables will be used to measure (operationalization). Complex concepts and those that are key to the research design are usually conceptualized with greater rigor than are those that are simple or less key to the program or evaluation.

7. What three strategies of operationalization are mentioned in the text?

Three approaches to operationalization are (1) to develop separate measures for each dimension, (2) to develop a single set of measures that encompass the dimensions, or (3) to develop a single measure. These three strategies reflect a declining order of rigor.

8. What is the theorem of the interchangeability of indicators, and why is it important?

The theorem of the interchangeability of indicators states that if several measures are equally valid indicators of a concept, then any subset of these measures will be valid as well. In other words, there are many valid ways to measure a given concept. This theorem is important because it implies that the analyst's task is to choose one approach and then justify that that approach is a valid one.

9. What is an index variable?

An index variable is a variable that combines the values of other variables into a single indicator or score. Index variables are commonly used to empirically measure abstract concepts and multifaceted phenomena.

10. How are index variables constructed?

Index variables are constructed by summing the values of variables that measure distinct, though related, aspects of the concept. When a value of one or more measurement variable(s) is missing, the respective value of the index variable is also missing. (See Table 3.2 in the textbook for an example.)

11. Name four strategies for validating index variables.

First, analysts argue that their measurement variables are reasonable from a theoretical perspective (that is, they have content validity). Second, they show that, empirically, index measures have an appropriate range of values. Third, they show that the variables are correlated with each other (that is, they have high internal reliability). Fourth, index variables can be compared with other known measures, derived from external (other studies) or internal (the same study) sources. Respectively, these are referred to as criterion and construct validity.

12. What is Cronbach alpha? What values are acceptable?

Cronbach alpha, also called measure alpha, is a measure of internal reliability. This is the extent to which measurement variables are correlated with each other. Variables that measure the same concept are assumed to correlate with each other. Alpha values between 0.80 and 1.00 are considered good, values between 0.70 and 0.80 are acceptable, and values below 0.70 are poor and indicate a need for analysts to consider a different mix of measurement variables that measure their concept.

CRITICAL THINKING

1. Explain the following statement: "Scales should encompass all of the possible values that a variable can assume."

_____

_____

_____

_____

_____

2. Explain the following statement. "Continuous-level scales are preferred over ordinal-level scales, which in turn are preferred over nominal-level scales."

_____

_____

_____

_____

_____

_____

_____

3. Explain how measurement scales (for example, Likert scales) can affect the phrasing of survey questions.

_____

_____

_____

_____

_____

_____

_____

4. The text states that "no correct number of dimensions or variables exist, only bad or lacking ones." Explain this statement.

_____

_____

_____

_____

_____

_____

_____

5. The text distinguishes three approaches to operationalization. When should the most rigorous approach be used? When should the least rigorous approach be used?

_____

_____

_____

_____

_____

_____

_____

6. A study wishes to measure "citizen trust in government" through the number of lawsuits filed against the federal government. Evaluate the measurement validity of this approach.

_____

_____

_____

_____

_____

_____

7. Explain the theorem of the interchangeability of indicators.

_____
_____
_____
_____
_____
_____

8. Explain the following statement: "When one or more of the measurement variables are missing from an observation, the value of the index variables for that observation is missing, too." What are the pros and cons of guessing the values of missing observations? Why should this not be done?

_____
_____
_____
_____
_____
_____

9. Explain the following concepts, and give an example of each: (1) face validity, (2) construct validity, (3) criterion validity, and (4) content validity.

_____
_____
_____
_____
_____
_____

10. Explain the following statement: "Analysts usually collect a few more variables than are minimally needed because they cannot know, prior to reliability analysis, which variable mix will have a sufficiently high alpha score to lend empirical support for the index measure."

_____
_____
_____
_____
_____
_____

APPLICATION EXERCISES

1. Examine the citizen survey in the documentation for the Public Perceptions dataset, in Chapter 21 of this workbook. What level of measurement scale is used for the different items?

_____
_____
_____
_____

2. Give some examples of nominal-, ordinal-, interval-, and ratio-level variables in your area of interest.

_____

_____

_____

_____

_____

3. An analyst wishes to measure public support for a new welfare program. (1) Develop some suitable measures using Likert items on a survey. (2) Show how incomplete, ambiguous, and overlapping scales create problems of measurement validity.

_____

_____

_____

_____

_____

4. A survey of citizens assesses the extent to which they perceive that the federal government works democratically. A second study measures the extent to which the governments of different countries are democratic. Conceptualize democracy in each of these two study contexts.

_____

_____

_____

_____

_____

5. Develop an index variable to measure "fear of statistics" among students in public and nonprofit management. Then develop an index variable to measure a concept in your area of interest.

_____

_____

_____

_____

_____

6. Select a sample of six Government Accountability Office reports (see Box 2.1 in the text) or scholarly articles that use empirical data. Examine how these reports or articles address the matter of measurement validity.

_____

_____

_____

_____

_____

7. **Develop some measures that might be used in a study that assesses a neighborhood crime control program. Discuss some challenges of measurement validity, as well as strategies for dealing with these challenges.**

_____

_____

_____

_____

_____

FURTHER READING

Conceptualization and measurement are typically discussed in books on research methods and program evaluation, and readers are referred to those mentioned in Chapter 2 of this workbook.

It is instructive to consider articles that show different approaches to operationalizing study concepts. An example of the first approach to operationalization discussed in the text (measures of different dimensions combined in separate indices and subsequently aggregated into a "super" index) is E. Berman and J. West, "Managing Emotional Intelligence in U.S. Cities: A Study of Public Managers," _Public Administration Review_ 68 (2008): 742–758. This article shows how "emotional intelligence" is conceptualized using four dimensions: self-awareness, self-management, social awareness, and relationship management. Each of these dimensions is subsequently operationalized. For example, the dimension of "self-awareness" is measured by the following survey items: managers who report to me (i) are able to express their feelings accurately, (ii) recognize the impact of their feelings on their actions, (iii) are clear about their personal, guiding values, (iv) know their strengths and limitations with certainty, and (v) are attuned to their feelings. The article provides the rationale for these survey items. The scientific literature is full of such examples on a broad range of topics, including environmental sustainability, organizational inclusion, neighborhood safety, and the like. Many articles also validate their index measures such as through triangulation. You may want to research your library's resources for articles that show indexes in your area of interest.

CHAPTER

4

Measuring and Managing Performance: Present and Future

Q & A

1. What is performance measurement?

Performance measurement provides a real-time assessment of what a program is doing, what resources it is using, and what it has accomplished recently. As an analytical process, it is designed to produce such information on an ongoing basis; it provides a snapshot that integrates important, frequently quantitative information about programs and policies. Performance measurement helps managers improve program monitoring and accountability and, by focusing on measurable results, improve program performance and stakeholder satisfaction, too.

2. How is performance measurement related to program evaluation?

Whereas program evaluation focuses on the past (what has a program or policy achieved?), performance measurement focuses on the present (what is a program or policy achieving?). Performance measurement developed from program evaluation. While thorough, program evaluation can be quite cumbersome and hence may produce information that is neither ongoing nor timely for management purposes. By contrast, performance measurement aims to be an up-to-date management information system.

3. What is the logic model?

The logic model is a way of conceptualizing program performance that shows relationships among inputs, activities, outputs, outcomes, and goals. (See the textbook for a schematic model.)

4. What is the difference between outputs and outcomes?

Outputs are the immediate, direct results of program activities. Outcomes are specific changes in behaviors or conditions that are measures of goal attainment.

5. What problem of measurement validity is mentioned in the text in connection with performance measurement, and how is it addressed?

Performance measures should avoid problems of inaccurate or incomplete measurement. In practice, performance measures do have these problems, and managers need to be clear about what their performance measures include and what they do not. Performance measures are best regarded as indicators only, to be used in conjunction with other, often qualitative information about programs and policies.

6. What is effectiveness?

Effectiveness is the level of results of a program or treatment. It is typically measured by one or more output or outcome measures.

7. *What is efficiency?*

Efficiency is the unit cost to produce a good or service. It is calculated as the output or outcomes over inputs, or O/I. Efficiency indicators can be calculated in different ways and should reflect program management concerns.

8. *What are workload ratios?*

Workload ratios are the ratios of activities over inputs, or A/I. For example, a workload ratio is the number of students in anger management courses per teacher providing such courses. Distinguishing between workload ratios and efficiency measures is important: a high caseload of clients does not mean that they are being served well.

9. *What are benchmarks?*

Benchmarks are standards against which performance is measured. Internal benchmarks are standards that organizations select based on what their own prior programs have achieved, or on what they feel is appropriate. External benchmarks are standards that are set based on the performance of other organizations and programs.

10. *What are equity measures?*

Equity measures are used to compare performance across different groups. Often, outputs and outcomes measures can be analyzed for different populations, types of organizations, and the like.

11. *What is performance management?*

Performance management is generally defined as activities to ensure that goals are consistently being met in an effective and efficient manner. Activities include using performance measures for improving accountability, service delivery, and managerial decision making, which is our focus here. Performance analysis is used in performance management to gain an understanding of program performance and the factors affecting it.

12. *What is forecasting? How is it related to planning?*

A forecast is a prediction about the future. This is sometimes also called a projection or prognosis. Forecasting is different from planning; whereas forecasting discusses what the future will look like, planning provides a normative model of what the future should look like. Planning often starts with forecasting to establish what the future is likely to look like, in order to develop alternative futures or scenarios that might be preferred.

13. *How are statistical methods used for forecasting?*

Statistical methods typically describe and aim to extrapolate quantitative trends based on past and present data. Analysis can involve no more than the simple extrapolation of the past few data points, but it can also analyze complex cyclical patterns and model other variables affecting past and present levels.

14. *What are judgment-based methods of forecasting?*

Judgment-based methods of forecasting often use experts to assess the likelihood of futures occurring. Experts can be brought together in groups, or as individuals. For example, the Delphi method is a forecasting method that asks experts to respond anonymously through several rounds of written surveys.

15. *What are some key practices and standards for making forecasts?*

Forecasts are more reliable for shorter periods; forecasting should use multiple methods; data and experts should be as up-to-date and valid as possible; forecasts should use as much information as possible about the past, present, and future; assumptions and limitations should be stated clearly; the accuracy of forecasts should be determined wherever possible; forecasts of more complex methods are not always more accurate than simple ones; forecasting should begin by identifying a full range of possible future scenarios and events; forecasting should note unusual past events that affect past data and adjust forecasts or the data accordingly; and forecasters should expect their forecasts to be challenged.

CRITICAL THINKING

1. How is a system of key indicators such as performance measurement different from a system of comprehensive measurement?

_____

_____

_____

_____

_____

_____

2. Explain how performance measurement provides useful information about programs and policies, even if it is not free from measurement errors.

_____

_____

_____

_____

_____

_____

3. Is the number of arrests by police officers an activity, an output, or an outcome? Explain your answer.

_____

_____

_____

_____

_____

_____

4. Give an example of the distinction between efficiency and a workload ratio not mentioned in the text.

_____

_____

_____

_____

_____

_____

5. Examine the measures in Table 4.1 in the textbook. Can you improve on these? Can you identify other measures? In what way might inaccurate or incomplete data affect these measures?

_____

_____

_____

_____

_____

6. What practical problems can you foresee in using external benchmarks? Can these problems be over-come? If so, how?

_____

_____

_____

_____

_____

_____

7. Explain how equity measures are important, especially in the context of public management.

_____

_____

_____

_____

_____

_____

8. Explain how performance management uses performance measurement to improve program perfor-mance. Give a few examples from your area of interest.

_____

_____

_____

_____

_____

_____

9. Explain the following statement: "Experts can help identify future events that trend forecasting may overlook." Give an example.

_____

_____

_____

_____

_____

_____

10. Discuss the following statement: "The accuracy of forecasts should be determined, such as by com-paring predictions about the present against the observed reality of the present."

_____

_____

_____

_____

_____

APPLICATION EXERCISES

1. Identify outputs and outcomes of a program to increase high school student graduation rates through homework assistance for at-risk students.

   _____
   _____
   _____
   _____
   _____

2. Identify outputs and outcomes of a program to reduce traffic congestion by adding dedicated bus lanes (lanes that only buses can use).

   _____
   _____
   _____
   _____
   _____

3. Develop a complete performance measurement system for a program or policy in your area of interest. Identify inputs, activities, outputs, outcomes, and goals, as well as measures of effectiveness, efficiency, and equity. See Table 4.1 in the textbook to get you started. You will want to add efficiency, effectiveness, and equity.

   _____
   _____
   _____
   _____
   _____

4. Research and compare examples of performance measurement in agencies in your area of interest. How similar are their measures? Can you explain the differences?

   _____
   _____
   _____
   _____
   _____

5. Look for examples of performance measurement and balanced scorecards on the Internet.

   _____
   _____
   _____
   _____
   _____

6. **Identify some statistical forecasts in your area of interest. What assumptions do they make? How might they be improved?**

   _____

   _____

   _____

   _____

   _____

   _____

7. **Develop some scenario-based forecasts in your area of interest.**

   _____

   _____

   _____

   _____

   _____

   _____

FURTHER READING

For a practical discussion on performance measurement, see H. Hatry, _Performance Measurement: Getting Results_, 2nd ed. (Washington, D.C.: Urban Institute, 2007). Another oft-used source is International City/County Management Association, _A Guide to Results-Oriented Government and Performance Measurement_ (Washington, D.C.: International City/County Management Association, 2004). Many jurisdictions have adapted this guide for their training purposes and have posted this information online (for example, www.miamidade.gov/mppa/library/reading_list/PerfMeasGuide-VMS.pdf). A primer on performance measurement can also be found at http://planning.utah.gov/PerformanceMeasurePrimer.html. Performance measurement is a basic competency, indeed, and applications also exist for nonprofit management: R. Penna, _The Nonprofit Outcomes Toolbox: A Complete Guide to Program Effectiveness, Performance Measurement, and Results_ (New York: Wiley, 2011). The classic work is H. Hatry et al., _How Effective Are Your Community Services? Procedures for Measuring Their Quality_ (Washington, D.C.: Urban Institute, 1992).

Although many books discuss forecasting methods, most of these books are for business, for example, J. Scott Armstrong, _Principles of Forecasting: A Handbook for Researchers and Practitioners_ (Norwell, Mass.: Kluwer, 2002). Many policy analysis books include some chapters on forecasting, such as Dipak K. Gupta, _Analyzing Public Policy: Concepts, Tools, and Techniques_, 2nd ed. (Washington, D.C.: CQ Press, 2010). Another such book is William Dunn, _Public Policy Analysis: An Introduction_, 4th ed. (New York: Longman, 2009). However, these chapters often provide little more than a very brief overview of the field.

CHAPTER
5

Data Collection

Q & A

1. What are administrative data, and for what purposes are they used?

Administrative data are generated in the course of managing programs and activities. Traditionally, administrative data are used to (1) ensure that resources are not misused, (2) monitor the status of activities, and (3) provide a record of what has been completed and accomplished. Today, administrative data are also collected to (4) meet the needs of performance measurement. These purposes may also be necessary for grant or contract compliance.

2. What are secondary data, and for what purposes are they used?

Secondary data are data that have been collected by other agencies for their own purposes but that are available to managers and may be relevant for their purposes. Secondary data can provide important information about communities and can be useful for needs assessment, benchmarking, and outcome measurement. Managers and analysts are expected to be familiar with the secondary data in their fields.

3. What types of surveys are mentioned in the text, and for what purposes are surveys used?

The four types of surveys are mail, Internet, phone, and in-person surveys. Surveys are commonly used in program evaluation research and, increasingly, performance measurement. Surveys are increasingly used when such knowledge needs to be quantitative, comprehensive, and systematic.

4. Discuss the pros and cons of different types of surveys. Why are phone surveys used increasingly?

Mail surveys allow for the most survey items, but the need for follow-up mailings increases the duration of data collection. Internet surveys have few survey items, and the lack of a sampling frame can pose problems. Phone surveys have important speed advantages but may have low response rates. In-person surveys offer the highest response rate but also carry the highest cost. Phone surveys are used increasingly because they can be completed in a short time and can be used to ask many questions.

5. List some standards for writing survey questions.

Survey questions should be clear (unambiguous and specific) and easy to answer. They should avoid double-barreled and leading questions. And they should avoid negative statements.

6. Explain the limitations and uses of customer comment cards.

Customer comment cards generate samples that are typically not representative of all customers, and therefore, they are not generalizable. They are useful, however, for obtaining feedback about problems that might need attention.

7. Which sources of data, other than administrative records and surveys, are mentioned in the text?

The chapter mentions trained observers, actors, experts, and focus groups.

8. What is a census?

A census is a survey or count (tally) of an entire group or population.

9. Why is obtaining a representative sample important? How is it different from a purposive sample?

Only representative samples allow for generalization to the population. Representative samples have a mix of characteristics similar to that of the population from which they are drawn, whereas purposive samples have an unrepresentative mix of characteristics (for example, "exemplary practices" surveys are often purposive samples). Some threats to validity for surveys are inadequate sampling frames and unrepresentative samples.

10. What is random sampling, and why is it important?

Random sampling is a sampling method whereby each member of the population has an equal chance of being selected for the sample. Random sampling is the most valid way of making representative samples.

11. Define sampling error. Do small or large samples have small sampling errors? Why?

The sampling error is the percentage by which sample findings vary in 95 of 100 repeated samples. Large samples better reflect population characteristics and thus have smaller sampling errors.

12. What is nonresponse bias?

Nonresponse bias occurs when the views of nonrespondents are different from those of respondents, thus affecting the generalizability of the sample.

13. Explain data coding, data input, and data cleaning.

Data coding is the process of preparing data (from pen-and-paper surveys or electronic or other sources) for input into statistical software programs. Data input (also, data entry) is the activity of recording these data in statistical software programs. Data cleaning is the process of identifying and removing reporting and recording errors. Errors include mistyped values, errors that arise in the process of uploading, and other implausible values that have been recorded. It is common practice to assume that unexamined data usually contain various errors that must be identified and removed.

CRITICAL THINKING

1. Identify some examples of the use of administrative data.

_____
_____
_____
_____
_____
_____

2. Identify and discuss problems in the quality of administrative data.

_____
_____
_____
_____
_____
_____

3. Identify some examples of the use of secondary data.

_____

_____

_____

_____

_____

_____

4. Identify and discuss problems in the quality of secondary data.

_____

_____

_____

_____

_____

_____

5. Contrast the use of systematic surveys and focus groups. For which purposes is each best suited? Give some examples.

_____

_____

_____

_____

_____

_____

6. Consider the following statement: "Our city is larger than the city next door, so we need a larger sample size for doing our citizen survey." Is this statement valid? Why, or why not?

_____

_____

_____

_____

_____

_____

7. Discuss the following statement: "Over 50 items can be asked when questions (in phone surveys) are easy and asked in a similar format." Find an example on the CD that accompanies this workbook.

_____

_____

_____

_____

_____

_____

8. Explain the concept of sampling error and why it matters.

_____

_____

_____

_____

_____

9. What practical problems do you see with drawing a random sample of all Americans as opposed to a random sample of those that live in your city?

_____

_____

_____

_____

_____

_____

10. Discuss why customer comment cards do not constitute a generalizable customer satisfaction survey.

_____

_____

_____

_____

_____

_____

11. Identify threats to validity arising from biased questions and sampling in surveys.

_____

_____

_____

_____

_____

_____

12. Explain the following statement: "It is common practice to assume that unexamined data usually contain various errors." Give some examples.

_____

_____

_____

_____

_____

_____

13. Identify four specific ways in which data that have not been thoroughly cleaned may be problematic.

_____

_____

_____

_____

_____

_____

APPLICATION EXERCISES

1. Identify administrative data in your field of interest. How can such data be used for managing programs?

   _____
   _____
   _____
   _____
   _____

2. Critique the validity of administrative data in your field of interest. How might the quality of administrative data be improved?

   _____
   _____
   _____
   _____
   _____

3. Identify secondary data in your field of interest. For what purposes might these be used?

   _____
   _____
   _____
   _____
   _____

4. Discuss how trained observers, actors, experts, and focus groups might be used in your field of interest.

   _____
   _____
   _____
   _____
   _____

5. Identify how client and citizen surveys might be used in your field of interest.

   _____
   _____
   _____
   _____
   _____

6. Use the Internet to find examples of client and citizen surveys in your field of interest. Then evaluate the (1) validity and (2) usefulness of these surveys.

   _____
   _____
   _____
   _____
   _____

7. Evaluate and improve the following survey question: "Please tell me whether you like living at your present location or would consider moving to another city."

_____

_____

_____

_____

_____

8. Develop some other poor survey questions, and then improve them. Use a Likert scale (see Chapter 3).

_____

_____

_____

_____

_____

9. Develop a survey of clients, citizens, or employees in your field of interest.

_____

_____

_____

_____

_____

10. Examine the methods section in the survey report on the CD that accompanies this workbook. Examine carefully how concerns about representative samples are dealt with.

_____

_____

_____

_____

_____

From Data Coding to Data Analysis

Below is a checklist of items for getting your data in order.

1. Does the dataset include all the observations (for example, respondents)?

2. Does the dataset include all the variables?

3. Has a sample of the dataset been compared against the actual observations for accuracy?

4. Do the variable names make sense?

5. Does each variable have a label (if needed)?

6. Does each variable value have a label (if needed)?

7. Have variable values that indicate a missing value been coded as missing?

8. Has each variable been checked for implausible values (including outliers)?

9. Have implausible values been corrected or omitted?

10. Do the ranges of variables make sense? Which variables have limited ranges, and what implications follow for subsequent analysis?

FURTHER READING

The leading text on survey research is Don Dillman et al., *Internet, Mail and Mixed-Mode Surveys: The Total Design Method,* 3rd ed. (New York: Wiley, 2008). For conducting citizen surveys for administrative purposes, see Thomas Miller and Michele Miller, *Citizen Surveys for Local Government: A Comprehensive Guide,* 3rd ed. (Washington, D.C.: International City/County Management Association, 2008). A book on public opinion polling from a political perspective is Herbert Asher, *Polling and the Public: What Every Citizen Should Know,* 7th ed. (Washington, D.C.: CQ Press, 2007). A classic book on issues with secondary data sources is Mark Maier, *The Data Game,* 3rd ed. (Armonk, N.Y.: M. E. Sharpe, 1999). Despite the publication date, this book contains authoritative discussions about the quality of secondary data in different fields of interest, such as demography, housing, health, education, crime, the economy, labor, and business. These chapters are essential reading for anyone dealing with secondary data in these specific fields.

Few separate articles or books deal with data cleaning. On the Internet, visit http://paul.rutgers.edu/~weiz/readinglist.html. Some books on data mining, which deals with getting information from large databases, discuss the importance of data cleaning. Some scholarly articles draw attention to problems with data, though these books often are quite sophisticated. In the end, the message is clear: we need to get our data in shape by trying to detect errors.

Central Tendency

Note to students: This chapter includes questions and exercises relating to the textbook introduction to Section III (Descriptive Statistics), indicated by SI (Section Introduction).

Q & A

1. What are descriptive statistics? Give some examples. (SI)

Descriptive statistics provide summary information about variables, such as their average and frequency distribution.

2. What is the distinction between univariate and bivariate analysis? (SI)

Univariate analysis describes single variables, whereas bivariate analysis examines the relationship between two variables.

3. What are some important tasks of analysts engaged in statistics?

Some important tasks of analysts engaged in statistics are as follows: (1) understanding the definition and purpose of a statistic, (2) ensuring that a statistic is appropriate to the data and problem at hand, (3) understanding the test assumptions of a statistic, (4) applying a statistic to the problem at hand in ways that are mindful of the preceding points, (5) drawing correct conclusions, and (6) communicating results in ways that are appropriate for both professional and general audiences.

4. What are variables? What are scales?

Variables are succinctly defined as empirically observable phenomena that vary (see Chapter 2 in the text). Scales are the collection of specific attributes (or values) used to measure a specific variable (see Chapter 3 in the text). There are four levels of measurement scales: nominal, ordinal, interval, and ratio. You need to be familiar with these concepts, as they are key to choosing the correct statistic.

5. What role does the measurement level play in univariate analysis?

The type of univariate statistics that should be used depends on the level of measurement.

6. Name the three measures of central tendency. How is each defined?

The three measures of central tendency are mean, median, and mode. The mean is the sum of a series of observations, divided by the number of observations in the series. The median is the middle value in a series (or array) of values that have been ordered from low to high. The mode is the most frequent (typical) value(s) of a variable.

7. How should analysts deal with the problem of missing data in calculating statistics?

The most common approach is to exclude such observations from calculations.

8. What is a weighted mean? For what purposes is it sometimes used?

The weighted mean is defined as a mean for which the observations have been given variable weights. Weighted means are commonly used to adjust for over- and undersampling in surveys, for example.

9. What is the formula for determining the location of the median?

The location of the median is determined by the formula $(n + 1)/2$. For example, if there are 97 observations, the median is the value of the 49th observation, when observations have been ordered. When there are 98 observations, the median is the mean of the 49th and 50th observations.

10. When should both the mean and median be used? When should the mode be used?

The median should be reported along with the mean when a few very large or very small observations affect the value of the mean. The mode is used infrequently, but an advantage of the mode is that it can be used with nominal-level data, which is not possible for calculating the mean or median.

CRITICAL THINKING

1. **Give some examples of univariate and bivariate analyses. (SI)**

_____

_____

_____

_____

_____

_____

2. **Why is the mean frequently used?**

_____

_____

_____

_____

_____

_____

3. **Consider the following statement: "Calculating the mean is straightforward, but managers and analysts may encounter some practical issues that, for the most part, concern the data rather than the formula itself." Give examples of these practical issues.**

_____

_____

_____

_____

_____

_____

4. Why are observations with missing values typically removed before calculating specific statistics?

_____

_____

_____

_____

_____

_____

5. Discuss the challenge of using the mean for calculating the central tendency of an ordinal-level variable (for example, a survey question that uses a Likert scale; see Box 3.1 in the text).

_____

_____

_____

_____

_____

_____

6. Explain the following statement: "The median should always be used when a few very large or very small values affect estimates of the mean." Give some examples of variables for which the median is typically used.

_____

_____

_____

_____

_____

_____

7. Explain the following statement: "An advantage of the mode is that it can be used with nominal-level data, which is not possible for calculating the mean or median."

_____

_____

_____

_____

_____

_____

DATA-BASED EXERCISES

1. Although computer software is used to calculate statistics, some students find that hand calculation furthers their conceptual understanding. Consider the following values: 4, 5, 7, 9, 11, 13, 13, 16, 18. Calculate the mean, median, and mode. After completing the exercise below, you might return to your results and verify them using the computer. (To practice, you can make up your own data, too.)

Mean: $\sum x_i/n =$ _____

Median: Value of observation at location $(n + 1)/2$: _____

Mode: Most frequent value: _____

2. **This is an exercise in data input. Data input is a skill that is specific to the software package you are using. Chapter 20 provides data input examples for SPSS. Input the data shown in the workbook Screen W20.4, and use SPSS to calculate the mean, median, and mode. Verify your results with those shown in Screen W20.8.**

3. **This is an exercise in data coding and input. Input the data from Table W6.1 into your statistical software program. For simplicity, the table shows only three respondent records of the three survey items. Note that respondent number 3 did not answer the first question. This needs to be coded as missing. Code this value as a "9" and instruct your statistical software to treat this value as missing. Also, create variable and value labels, as shown in Screens W20.3 and W20.4.**

Table W6.1 ———～～— Selected Data from Three Survey Respondents

How important are the following issues for you? Please state whether you consider each issue Very Important, Important, Somewhat Important, or Unimportant:

Respondent 1:

	Very Important	Important	Somewhat Important	Unimportant
Controlling government spending	[ ]	[x]	[ ]	[ ]
Cutting property taxes	[x]	[ ]	[ ]	[ ]
Reducing I-4 congestion	[ ]	[x]	[ ]	[ ]

Respondent 2:

	Very Important	Important	Somewhat Important	Unimportant
Controlling government spending	[ ]	[x]	[ ]	[ ]
Cutting property taxes	[ ]	[ ]	[ ]	[x]
Reducing I-4 congestion	[x]	[ ]	[ ]	[ ]

Respondent 3:

	Very Important	Important	Somewhat Important	Unimportant
Controlling government spending	[ ]	[ ]	[ ]	[ ]
Cutting property taxes	[x]	[ ]	[ ]	[ ]
Reducing I-4 congestion	[x]	[ ]	[ ]	[ ]

4. **Read about the Community Indicators dataset in Chapter 21 of this workbook. Then open this dataset using your statistical software package (for example, SPSS). Compare the mean and median values of the number of murders ("Murder") in these different cities. Are the values of the mean and median similar or dissimilar? Calculate the mean and median of other variables of your choice, too. In Chapter 7, we will take this analysis further by making frequency distributions.**

_____

_____

_____

_____

_____

5. **A local government operates a small park near to its city hall. The department uses the attendance to measure its workload in determining the budget for the park. The city manager has long believed that the park has too few visitors and that the department should reach out to more customers or its budget will need to be reduced. You are an analyst for the city. The city manager has asked you to prepare an analysis for the park to determine whether the budget request for the park is justified in the city's budget proposal. You randomly selected 25 days in the past year and calculated the park attendance data: 5, 3, 10, 1, 2, 3, 4, 3, 5, 100, 4, 3, 2, 4, 25, 150, 3, 3, 5, 4, 8, 7, 10, 15, and 30.**

   a. Use computer software (SPSS or Excel) to calculate the mean, the median, and the mode for the data. Write a paragraph to explain the meaning of these statistics. Do you recommend the use of the mean in your presentation? Why or why not? Do you recommend the use of the median or the mode? Why or why not?

   b. (*optional*) Prepare a report to discuss recommendations to the city manager.

   _____
   _____
   _____
   _____
   _____

6. **Using the Community Indicators dataset, calculate the mean burglary rate per capita. To do this, you first need to create a new variable, which is the burglary rate per capita for each city in the dataset. Let's call this variable "burglaryrate" and define it as burglary/pop, whereby "burglary" and "pop" correspond to the variable names in the Community Indicators dataset. Use your statistical software program to calculate the mean and median burglary rates per capita. Which three cities have the highest burglary rates per capita? Are these the same cities as those with the largest number of burglaries?**

   _____
   _____
   _____
   _____
   _____

   Note for students using SPSS: See Screen W20.2. Type "burglaryrate" (without quotes) in the target variable field, and type "burglary/pop" (without quotes) in the numeric expression field. Select OK and see the new variable created in your Data Editor screen. It will have been added at the end of the existing variables, all the way to the right in the Data View screen, or at the end of the list in the Variable View screen. You may want to change the number of decimals shown to, say, five (5); see Screen W20.3 for this purpose.

7. **Open the Watershed dataset and read the description of this survey in workbook Chapter 21. Calculate the mean and the median of the number of samples that exceed pollution standards (Conpolut) and fish and wildlife advisories (Advisory).**

   _____
   _____
   _____
   _____
   _____

8. (*optional*) **Consider the table of grouped data (Table W6.2). Calculate the grouped mean and grouped median. (see Chapter 6 appendix)**

Table W6.2 ⎯⎯⎯⎯⎯∿∿⎯ Frequency Table

Category	Interval of variable "x"	Frequency	Cumulative frequency
1	1–4	33	33
2	5–8	47	80
3	8–11	64	144
4	12–15	32	176
5	16–19	14	190

Grouped Mean

Step 1: Calculate the weighted mean of categories:

_____

_____

_____

Step 2: Calculate the estimated value of the variable mean:

_____

_____

_____

Grouped Median

Step 1: Determine the location of the median:

_____

_____

_____

Step 2: Calculate the estimated value of the variable median:

_____

_____

_____

Note: Chapter 7 contains more introductory data-based exercises, such as involving frequency charts and frequency distributions. Many analyses, including exercises in data cleaning, involve the techniques discussed in that chapter.

FURTHER READING

The statistics described in this chapter are quite basic. A fun, introductory book to statistics is Larry Gonick and Woollcott Smith, *The Cartoon Guide to Statistics* (New York: Harper Perennial, 2008). It does a nice job of explaining statistical concepts and includes many of the statistics described in subsequent chapters. Somewhat less useful is Murray Spiegel and Larry Stephens, *Schaum's Outlines: Statistics,* 3rd ed. (New York: McGraw-Hill, 2007). It has chapters on descriptive statistics and other statistics discussed in this course, but the treatment is not very applied. Of course, you can consult many basic books on statistics, but few focus on public affairs. For example, R. Mark Sirkin, *Statistics for the Social Sciences,* 3rd ed. (Thousand Oaks, Calif.: Pine Forge Press, 2005) is written in an accessible style, and it emphasizes learning through understanding and application of mathematical calculations. Another option is Chava Frankfort-Nachmias and Anna Leon-Guerrero, *Social Statistics for a Diverse Society,* 6th ed. (Thousand Oaks, Calif.: Sage, 2010). The suggested readings in Chapter 2 related to the ethics of data analysis and presentation also provide useful advice on basic statistics, for example, Darrell Huff, *How to Lie with Statistics* (New York: Norton, 1993). An online source is www.statsoft.com/textbook/elementary-concepts-in-statistics/.

A good exercise on the road toward mastering concepts and applications in statistics is to view their use in scholarly research and professional practice. For example, read some issues of leading academic journals and note their use of descriptive statistics. Some of the leading journals in public affairs and political science are *American Political Science Review, Public Administration Review,* and *Journal of Public Policy Analysis and Management.* Of course, many good scholarly journals are available, and you might ask your professor for a reading list or even for specific articles highlighting the uses of statistics discussed in this and subsequent chapters.

If you are using SPSS and you want more information than is offered in Chapter 20 of this workbook, try the most recent version of *SPSS Base User's Guide* (Chicago: SPSS) for whatever version of SPSS you are using. Or you can call SPSS Inc., at 312-651-3000. You can also try Earl Babbie and Fred Halley, *Adventures in Social Research: Data Analysis Using SPSS,* 7th ed. (Thousand Oaks, Calif.: Pine Forge Press, 2010).

CHAPTER

7

Measures of Dispersion

Q & A

1. What are measures of dispersion?

Measures of dispersion provide information about how the values of a variable are distributed.

2. What are frequency distributions? What are they used for?

Frequency distributions describe the range and frequency of values of a variable. They are used for nominal- and ordinal-level data. Frequency distributions often are a prelude for generating data tables and attractive graphics and are also used for data cleaning.

3. What is a histogram? How is it different from a bar chart?

A histogram shows the number of observations in different categories (or values) of the variable. Analysts can define the number (or widths) of categories that are used to group the different values of the variable. Bar charts are similar, but they show the number of observations for each different value of the variable. By convention, histograms are used for continuous variables, and bar charts are used for categorical variables.

4. Discuss the use of bar charts, pie charts, and line graphs.

Bar charts show the frequency of occurrences through stacks, which can be used to highlight the importance of categories (values). Bar charts are used with ordinal- or nominal-level variables. Pie charts typically are used to focus on equality: Who gets most (or least) of what? Pie charts are used with nominal-level variables. Line graphs are usually used for continuous variables, partly to avoid displaying a large number of bars.

5. What is an outlier? How are they dealt with?

Outliers are analyst-defined observations with unusual values relative to other values in the data. Outliers are defined as observations whose values are either less than the inner fence or greater than the outer fence. Outliers may be the result of data-coding errors or reflect actual but unusual values in the sample. The textbook suggests that observations that are flagged as outliers generally should be retained when they are not coding errors, when they are plausible values of the variable in question, and when they do not greatly affect the value of the mean (of continuous variables).

6. What is the standard deviation?

The standard deviation is a measure of dispersion that is calculated based on the values of the data.

7. What statistical property makes the standard deviation a desirable statistic?

When data are normally distributed, 68.3 percent of the observations lie within ±1 standard deviation from the mean, 95.4 percent lie ±2 standard deviations from the mean, and 99.7 percent lie ±3 standard deviations from the mean.

8. How do analysts determine whether a variable is normally distributed?

Some analysts rely on a visual inspection, aided by a computer-generated curve that is superimposed over the histogram. Analysts also use measures of skewness and kurtosis to determine whether the shape of the observed curve is consistent with a normal distribution. Sample data are not expected to match a theoretical bell-shaped curve perfectly because of deviations due to chance selection.

9. What are standardized variables?

Standardized variables (also called z-scores) are variables that have been transformed such that their means are exactly 0 and their standard deviations are exactly 1 (or unity).

10. (optional) What is a boxplot? For what purpose is it used? (Chapter 7 appendix)

A boxplot is a graphical device that shows various measures of dispersion. Boxplots are useful for obtaining a quick, visual, preliminary understanding of data; they are useful tools for data cleaning. Statistics associated with boxplots are calculated based on the location of data.

CRITICAL THINKING

1. Explain why frequency distributions are widely used.

_____

_____

_____

_____

_____

_____

2. Explain how frequency distributions can assist with data cleaning.

_____

_____

_____

_____

_____

_____

3. Explain the following statement: "When recoding variables or creating histograms, a practical question is how wide each category should be. To avoid perceptions of lying with statistics, a rule of thumb is that categories should be based on category ranges of equal length."

_____

_____

_____

_____

_____

_____

4. Describe the difference between a histogram, a bar chart, and a stem-and-leaf plot.

_____

_____

_____

_____

_____

_____

5. Research some innovative ways of using graphs to get your points across.

6. What percentage of observations has a higher z-score value than 0.86? What percentage of observations has a lower z-score value than −1.15? What useful questions can a z-score statistic help answer? Hint: In the normal distribution table (see Appendix A in the textbook), look up values of the absolute difference between the above z-score values and 0.50 (l0.5 − z-scorel).

_____

_____

_____

_____

_____

_____

7. *(optional)* What is the purpose of a boxplot? Is a boxplot fence an actual observation or a calculated number? What about a whisker? (Chapter 7 appendix)

_____

_____

_____

_____

_____

_____

8. *(optional)* Using Figure W7.1, draw a boxplot of a variable with these values: 4, 5, 7, 9, 11, 13, 13, 16, 18, and 24. Are there any outliers? Why, or why not? (Chapter 7 appendix)

Figure W7.1 ———⌇⌇— Application: Boxplot

DATA-BASED EXERCISES

1. Although the computer calculates statistics, some students find that hand calculation furthers their conceptual understanding. Consider the following values: 4, 5, 7, 9, 11, 13, 13, 16, 18. (These were also used in workbook Chapter 6, Data-Based Exercise 1.) Now, calculate the standard deviation. You can use the computer to verify your results.

Standard deviation: $\sqrt{\dfrac{\sum (x_i - \bar{x})^2}{n-1}}$

$$\bar{x} \quad : \quad \underline{\hspace{6cm}}$$

$$x_1 - \bar{x}: \underline{\hspace{3cm}} \qquad (x_1 - \bar{x})^2 : \underline{\hspace{3cm}}$$

$$x_2 - \bar{x}: \underline{\hspace{3cm}} \qquad (x_2 - \bar{x})^2 : \underline{\hspace{3cm}}$$

$$x_3 - \bar{x}: \underline{\hspace{3cm}} \qquad (x_3 - \bar{x})^2 : \underline{\hspace{3cm}}$$

$$x_4 - \bar{x}: \underline{\hspace{3cm}} \qquad (x_4 - \bar{x})^2 : \underline{\hspace{3cm}}$$

$$x_5 - \bar{x}: \underline{\hspace{3cm}} \qquad (x_5 - \bar{x})^2 : \underline{\hspace{3cm}}$$

$$x_6 - \bar{x}: \underline{\hspace{3cm}} \qquad (x_6 - \bar{x})^2 : \underline{\hspace{3cm}}$$

$$x_7 - \bar{x}: \underline{\hspace{3cm}} \qquad (x_7 - \bar{x})^2 : \underline{\hspace{3cm}}$$

$$x_8 - \bar{x}: \underline{\hspace{3cm}} \qquad (x_8 - \bar{x})^2 : \underline{\hspace{3cm}}$$

$$x_9 - \bar{x}: \underline{\hspace{3cm}} \qquad (x_9 - \bar{x})^2 : \underline{\hspace{3cm}}$$

$$\sum (x_i - \bar{x})^2 : \underline{\hspace{6cm}}$$

$$\sqrt{\dfrac{\sum (x_i - \bar{x})^2}{n-1}} \quad : \quad \underline{\hspace{6cm}}$$

2. **Standard deviation is a useful concept in performance management. It can be useful in performance comparison, performance monitoring, and performance evaluation. Let us say that a director in a local fire department wants to know any variation between the performance of this year and that of the last year. He draws a sample of 10 response times of this year (in minutes): 3.0, 12.0, 7.0, 4.0, 4.0, 6.0, 3.0, 9.0, 11.0, and 15.0, comparing them with a sample of 10 response times from last year (in minutes): 8.0, 7.0, 8.0, 6.0, 6.0, 9.0, 7.0, 9.0, 8.0, and 6.0.**

   a. Does he see a performance variation by the mean? _____

   b. Does he see a performance variation by the standard deviation? If he does, is it a performance improvement or a performance deterioration from the last year? Why?

      _____

      _____

   c. Now, imagine that you are a citizen receiving fire protection services from this local fire department. How do you evaluate the response times of this fire department, by the mean, by the standard deviation, or by both?

      _____

      _____

   d. If the average response time improves (shortens) but the standard deviation of the response times deteriorates (increases), what is your conclusion of the performance as a service recipient? In other words, do you want a quicker average response at the expense of a more unpredictable response? What is your recommendation to the director on which statistical measures he should use and how he should use them?

      _____

      _____

      _____

      _____

3. **This is an exercise in data cleaning. Prior to performing any type of data evaluation, you must first become familiar with the dataset and the nature of the variables you wish to evaluate. The first dataset is from a citizen survey performed in Orange County, Florida. Open the Public Perceptions dataset.**

   a. Read the description of this dataset, the methodology, the survey instrument, and notes regarding the variables and values.

   b. How many observations are contained within this dataset? _____

   c. How many variables are contained in the set? _____

   d. What are the measurement levels of the variables Gender, Age, and Yearsorc? Yearsorc measures the number of years that the respondent has lived in Orange County. Determining measurement levels is relevant to the selection of statistics later. The measurement level can be determined in many ways, for example, by making a frequency chart and examining the category values.

Gender: —————————————

Age: —————————————

Yearsorc: —————————————

e. We now examine whether the present variable values are plausible (that is, whether they make sense). Make a frequency distribution for the variable Yearsorc. Are these values plausible?

———————————————————————————————————————

f. (*optional*) To further validate your suspicions, make a boxplot of the variable Yearsorc. What do you conclude?

———————————————————————————————————————

———————————————————————————————————————

g. Let's remove this observation. It is quite unlikely that someone has actually lived 301 years in Orange County. It might be a coding error (or a practical joke), but in any event we are unable to obtain the correct value at this point. Note also that the revised boxplot still indicates some outliers. However, these are quite plausible values. We use our judgment and decide to retain them.

h. (*optional*) Run some boxplots on other variables to see if there are any outliers. Do you need to make any other changes?

———————————————————————————————————————

4. **According to the Public Perceptions survey, do residents feel that the county has done a good job of balancing growth with environmental concerns? Make a frequency distribution. The variable is named Balance. Also, construct two bar charts: one that includes all three categories, and one that omits the category "don't know."**

———————————————————————————————————————

———————————————————————————————————————

———————————————————————————————————————

———————————————————————————————————————

———————————————————————————————————————

5. **According to the Public Perceptions survey, how do residents feel about their service experience? Specifically, what percentage of respondents agree or strongly agree that employees were helpful? What percentage of respondents agree or strongly agree that service was provided in a timely manner?**

Note: Analyze data for only those respondents who stated that they have had contact with county employees during the last 12 months.

———————————————————————————————————————

———————————————————————————————————————

———————————————————————————————————————

———————————————————————————————————————

———————————————————————————————————————

6. **Among the items listed in section I of the Public Perceptions survey, which five items are the most important? Which items are the least important for residents? Based on what statistic do you decide this? What type of graph might you use to present your findings?**

———————————————————————————————————————

———————————————————————————————————————

———————————————————————————————————————

———————————————————————————————————————

———————————————————————————————————————

7. **Open the Community Indicators dataset. Examine the frequency distributions of the variables murder and nonnegligent manslaughter (called "Murder" on the dataset), burglary (called "Burglary"), and forcible rape (called "Rape"). Then use boxplots to determine whether any cities might be considered outliers among these measures. Based on your findings, should you include or exclude these cities from any further analysis? If you include them, should you note and study the impact that these cities have on your results?**

    _____
    _____
    _____
    _____
    _____

8. **The Employee Attitudes survey contains several items that reasonably might affect workplace performance. Read the description of this survey. How do employees feel about the following items: the morale among county employees, the extent that their organization welcomes change, receiving timely feedback about performance, and cooperation among departments? The variables are, respectively, Himorale, Welchang, Feedback, and Coopdept.**

    _____
    _____
    _____
    _____
    _____

9. **Open the Watershed dataset and read the description of the survey. Calculate the mean and median of the number of samples that exceed pollution standards (Conpolut) and fish and wildlife advisories (Advisory). Make a bar chart of the quality of watersheds (Wshedch).**

    _____
    _____
    _____
    _____
    _____

FURTHER READING

The readings discussed in Chapter 6 should help with the material here, too. Basic statistics books will discuss standard deviations, bar charts, and the like. Another useful book is Mark Berenson et al., *Basic Business Statistics*, 3rd ed. (Upper Saddle River, N.J.: Pearson Education, 2005).

Few separate articles or books deal with data cleaning. On the Internet, visit http://paul.rutgers. edu/~weiz/readinglist.html. Some books on data mining, which deals with getting information from large databases, discuss the importance of data cleaning. Some scholarly articles draw attention to problems with data, though these books often are quite sophisticated. In the end, the message is clear: we need to get our data in shape by trying to detect errors.

Graphical displays are increasingly used in presentations, of course. This may be a good time to familiarize yourself with standards of making presentations (for example, with PowerPoint) and the use of graphics. See, for example, Cliff Atkinson, *Beyond Bullet Points* (Redmond, Wash.: Microsoft Press, 2007). In addition, you might want to visit a website like www.smartdraw.com to become familiar with graphics and other visual representations.

CHAPTER
8

Contingency Tables

Q & A

1. What are bivariate statistics? How do bivariate analyses help managers and policymakers?

Bivariate statistics is the study of relationships among two variables. Providing empirical information about relationships is a key step in determining program effectiveness, and bivariate statistics can help managers and policymakers by determining how variables affect key outcomes.

2. What is a contingency table?

A contingency table expresses the relationship between two categorical variables. One variable is shown in rows and the other in columns. The cells show the number (and, often, percentages) of observations associated with specific values of the two categorical variables.

3. How does causality affect the design of contingency tables?

When bivariate relationships between two categorical variables are causal, the independent variable should be placed in the columns and the dependent variable in the rows. When relationships are associations, there is no preference concerning the placement of variables. Although this convention often is violated, following it makes the analysis of tables easier when column percentages are used, as is commonly the case.

4. How are column percentages calculated? How are they used for examining relationships?

Column percentages are calculated by dividing each frequency by the column total. Relationships in contingency tables are usually examined by comparing column percentages across (groups of) rows.

5. What are marginal totals?

Marginal totals are the row and column totals.

6. What is a statistical definition of a relationship?

A statistical relationship means that as one variable changes, so too, does another.

7. What is a positive relationship? What is a negative relationship?

Relationships involving ordinal or continuous variables are characterized as positive or negative. A positive relationship means that large values of one variable are associated with large values of the other variable and that small values of one variable are associated with small values of the other variable. A negative relationship implies the opposite: large values of one variable are associated with small values of the other variable, and vice versa.

8. What is a pivot table? How is it different from a contingency table?

Pivot tables show statistics of one or more continuous variables for one or more categorical variables in the data cells. By contrast, the cells of contingency tables show the number (and, often, percentages) of observations associated with specific values of the two categorical variables.

9. What is a layer variable?

A layer variable is one that defines the subset of data used for subsequent data tables.

10. What does the term transposing mean?

Transposing means interchanging the column and row variables; column variables become row variables, and vice versa.

CRITICAL THINKING

1. Identify all the features of contingency tables: title, clear column and row headings, data cell frequencies, column percentages, marginal totals, and grand total.

_____

_____

_____

_____

_____

_____

2. Explain the following statement: "Examining relationships in contingency tables is usually based on comparing column percentages for each or groups of rows." Give an example.

_____

_____

_____

_____

_____

_____

3. Calculate column percentages for Table W8.1:

Table W8.1 ⎯⎯⎯⎯⎯ Welfare Outcomes by Level of Education

Welfare outcome	Education		
	No H.S. degree	H.S. degree	Some college
Low	60	55	10
Medium	35	55	15
High	25	30	20

Note: H.S. = high school.

4. Practice writing up the results for the preceding question. Identify the number of recipients and how they differ by education and welfare outcome. Then discuss the relationships between these two variables. Use statements in the form of "Whereas xx percent of recipients with no high school degree

have high welfare outcomes, xx percent of recipients with some college have high welfare outcomes," and so on.

_____
_____
_____
_____
_____
_____

5. Explain how pivot tables and contingency tables are relevant to analysis of problems in your area of interest. Provide some examples.

_____
_____
_____
_____
_____
_____

6. Study the latest issues of research journals or professional reports in your field of interest; examine the use of tables and how the reports are written up. Record your findings on a separate sheet.

DATA-BASED EXERCISES

Note to students: The following exercises are designed to give you practice making contingency tables and pivot tables. However, because the interpretation of contingency tables is often difficult without the use of the statistics presented in Chapter 10, some of the write-up and interpretation regarding these tables is postponed until that chapter.

1. Use the Employee Attitudes dataset. Examine the relationship between gender and the morale of county employees (Himorale). Then consider the relationship between gender and stress (Stressed). Use column percentages, and write up the results.

_____
_____
_____
_____
_____

2. Use the Public Perceptions dataset. Consider the relationship between gender (Gender) and trusting the county government to do what is right most of the time (Trust). Is the difference between men and women large or small? Is it meaningful to describe the relationship as being positive or negative?

_____
_____
_____
_____
_____

3. Use the Public Perceptions dataset. The three most important issues are (see part I of the survey in Chapter 21) as follows: helping public schools (Pubschl), fighting illegal drug use (Figtdrug), and dealing with the problems of gangs (Gangs). Do whites and nonwhites agree on the importance of these priorities? On which issues is there a difference?

    _____

    _____

    _____

    _____

    _____

4. Use the Employee Attitudes dataset. A manager wishes to examine the relationship between race (Race) and perceptions that the people who get promoted are among the best qualified (Bestqual) in the Public Works Department. However, very few employees are minorities, and a manager is concerned that separate analysis for each minority group might reveal their identity. Therefore, the manager wants to compare Caucasian employees against non-Caucasian employees. Recode the variable Race in this manner, and report on the above relationship.

    _____

    _____

    _____

    _____

    _____

5. Use the Employee Attitudes dataset. Examine the relationship between the morale of county employees (Himorale) and being satisfied with one's job (Satisjob). Is this table easy or difficult to interpret?

    Note: The statistics discussed in Chapter 11 help to interpret whether a relationship exists between these two variables and, if so, whether it is positive or negative.

    _____

    _____

    _____

    _____

    _____

6. Open the Watershed dataset, and make a pivot table from variables in that dataset. For example, consider region and drinking water impairment as the two categorical variables, and show the mean level of conventional pollutants in each data cell. You may choose other continuous variables, as well.

    Note: See footnotes in Chapter 8 of the textbook for information on how to create pivot tables in SPSS and Excel.

    _____

    _____

    _____

    _____

    _____

7. Does class attendance affect a student's academic performance? To answer this question, you can conduct a study based on your personal experience. Consider all the classes you have taken in college. Code as ordinal variables your attendance in a course (for example, good or not so good) and your

academic performance (for example, A or not A). Conduct a contingency table analysis to examine the relationship between attendance (the independent variable) and academic performance (the dependent variable). Write a paragraph to report your finding.

_____

_____

_____

_____

_____

FURTHER READING

This chapter deals with contingency tables and pivot tables. Although no specialized texts cover these matters, user's manuals and published articles provide further reading. For example, the _SPSS 17.0 Base User's Guide_ (Upper Saddle River, N.J.: Prentice Hall, 2009 or later editions) has separate chapters on using contingency tables (called Crosstabs in SPSS) and pivot tables. This guide is also available online at http://support .spss.com/productsext/statistics/documentation/17.0.2/User%20Manuals/English/PASW%20Statistics%20 Base%20User's%20Guide%2017.0.pdf.

Many articles and reports show the use of contingency tables, and students can examine how these authors interpret and write up the results—almost every research journal has articles with contingency tables, of course. You can also visit the Government Accountability Office (GAO) website for examples of reports with tables (see www.gao.gov/browse/date/week).

CHAPTER

9

Getting Results

Q & A

1. What are analyses of outputs and outcomes? Can you give an example?

These are efforts that define, calculate, and display output and outcome measures of a program or an effort. The text discusses, as an example, outputs and outcomes related to a job training program. Outputs include the number of training sessions taught, whereas outcomes refer to trainees who find jobs.

2. What are analyses of efficiency and effectiveness? Can you give an example?

These are efforts that define, calculate, and display efficiency and effectiveness measures of a program or an effort. As an example, we can compare the costs to graduate each student in two schools (that is, cost/number of students graduated) to identify which school is more efficient by this measure. Effectiveness refers to outcomes such as the number of students graduated.

3. What are analyses of equity? Can you give an example?

These are efforts that define, calculate, and display how program resources, efforts, and outcomes vary across groups. These analyses may also concern matters of equal treatment across groups. As an example, we might assess the gender participation rates in a local government workforce over time to identify the trend in equal access to work opportunity.

4. What are quality-of-life analyses? Can you give an example?

A quality-of-life measurement is a composite index that assesses a variety of aspects in service or life quality of a community. A quality-of-life analysis is the effort to define, calculate, and display measures of the quality-of-life index of a community. As an example, we can create a quality-of-life index measure for an urban area that includes outcome measures in service areas such as public safety, health care, transportation, environmental protection, education, and other essential public services and specify the trend of the index by examining the values of the index over time.

CRITICAL THINKING

1. Explain the difference between performance measurement and performance management.

_____

_____

_____

_____

_____

_____

2. Give some examples of how statistical concepts and tools can enhance the application of performance measurement and performance management.

_____

_____

_____

_____

_____

_____

3. Consider the following expression: "What gets measured, gets done." Discuss the pros and cons of this approach to performance management.

_____

_____

_____

_____

_____

_____

4. What limitations would a manager face if he or she understood the concepts involved in performance measurement and performance management but did not have the ability to produce statistical analyses?

_____

_____

_____

_____

_____

_____

5. How is the application of statistics in performance measurement and performance management enhanced through the use of charts (that is, graphs and tables)? Conduct a simple experiment in which the results of a statistical analysis are presented to an audience with and without the use of charts. What differences does the presentation of charts make? Besides the visual enhancement provided, what other benefits do you see from presenting information using graphs and tables?

_____

_____

_____

_____

_____

_____

6. How is your understanding of statistical concepts enhanced by studying the analyses of outputs, outcomes, efficiency, and effectiveness in this chapter?

_____

_____

_____

_____

_____

7. Is your understanding of statistical concepts enhanced by studying the quality-of-life analyses in this chapter? Why or why not?

_____

_____

_____

_____

_____

_____

DATA-BASED EXERCISES

1. The department of transportation in a state government has four vehicle registration offices in a metropolitan area. The department recently conducted a series of studies to determine the number of mistakes made in issuing or renewing driver's licenses (an outcome measure). Twelve tests were conducted in each of these four offices, and the results are shown in Table W9.1.

Table W9.1 ⎯⎯⎯⎯⎯⎯ⱽⱽ⎯ Number of Errors in Vehicle License Offices (per 100 Licenses Issued)

	Office A	Office B	Office C	Office D
Test 1	3.00	6.00	9.00	9.00
Test 2	7.00	3.00	4.00	9.00
Test 3	8.00	2.00	2.00	7.00
Test 4	5.00	5.00	2.00	6.00
Test 5	5.00	2.00	6.00	4.00
Test 6	5.00	9.00	2.00	1.00
Test 7	1.00	6.00	10.00	2.00
Test 8	9.00	4.00	5.00	9.00
Test 9	10.00	8.00	6.00	10.00
Test 10	5.00	2.00	7.00	4.00
Test 11	3.00	2.00	7.00	1.00
Test 12	4.00	1.00	8.00	2.00

Calculate the mean, the sample variance, the sample standard deviation, the maximum, the minimum, and the range for each agency. Discuss the meaning of each of these performance measures for the agencies.

_____

_____

_____

_____

_____

2. Which agency has the best performance, based on these measures? Which has the worst? What makes you draw these conclusions? If the state decides to retrain agencies one at a time, what would be your priority list for retraining? Explain your rationale for creating this list.

_____

_____

_____

_____

3. Calculate the frequency and cumulative distributions for the number of errors for each agency. Let's say that the department's goal is for at least 50 percent of each agency's tests to find no more than five errors. Which agency or agencies meet this performance benchmark, and which don't? Explain your findings.

_____
_____
_____
_____
_____

4. Use five or fewer errors as a benchmark to categorize the test scores for each agency (that is, with categories of "five or fewer errors" and "more than five errors"). Perform a contingency table analysis for all four agencies. Discuss your findings.

_____
_____
_____
_____
_____

5. Practice making a few professional-looking charts using Microsoft Excel. Excel allows analysts to create different types of charts, including column charts, bar charts, pie charts, and line charts. To create a chart in Excel, click on the Insert tab and then select the chart type from the Charts group. You can modify charts, apply predefined styles and layouts, and add various formatting features. Chapter 19 of this workbook provides an example of how to create a chart using Excel.

FURTHER READING

See Chapter 4 of this workbook for many good sources regarding the performance measurement and management literature. More advanced discussions regarding the role of performance management in public management can be found in Carolyn Heinrich and Laurence Lynn (eds.), *Governance and Performance: New Perspectives* (Washington, D.C.: Georgetown University Press, 2000); Jeffrey Brudney, Laurence O'Toole, and Hal Rainey (eds.), *Advancing Public Management* (Washington, D.C.: Georgetown University Press, 2000); and George Boyne, Kenneth Meier, Laurence O'Toole, and Richard Walker (eds.), *Public Service Performance: Perspectives on Measurement and Management* (New York: Cambridge University Press, 2006). For more on the application of performance measurement, see David Ammons (ed.), *Leading Performance Management in Local Government* (Washington, D.C.: International City/County Management Association, 2008). For the application of statistical tools in performance management, see XiaoHu Wang, *Performance Analysis for Public and Nonprofit Organizations* (Burlington, Mass.: Jones and Bartlett, 2010).

Hypothesis Testing with Chi-Square

Q & A

Note to students: This chapter includes questions and exercises relating to the textbook introduction to Section IV (Inferential Statistics), indicated SI (Section Introduction).

1. What are inferential statistics? (SI)

Inferential statistics are statistics used to make inferences about characteristics in the population from which sample data were drawn. Most commonly, inferential statistics are used to determine, on the basis of a sample, whether a relationship exists in the population from which the sample data were drawn.

2. Name three types of bivariate tests. Explain when each should be used. (SI)

There are many statistical tests for bivariate data. The type of data (level of measurement) determines which statistical test should be used. The section introduction discusses the following:

- When two variables are categorical, tests based on contingency tables should be used.
- When one variable is dichotomous (for example, gender) and the other is continuous, the t-test should be used.
- When both variables are continuous, simple regression analysis should be used.

3. Which five steps are followed in deciding the statistical significance of relationships?

1. State the null hypothesis (in Greek letters).
2. Choose a statistical test.
3. Calculate the test statistic (t.s.), and evaluate test assumptions.
4. Look up the critical value (c.v.) of the test.
5. Draw conclusion: If |t.s.| < c.v., do not reject null hypothesis. If |t.s.| ≥ c.v., reject the null hypothesis.

4. Explain the purpose of stating the null hypothesis.

The purpose of stating the null hypothesis is to establish a reasonable ground that a relationship exists. By assuming that a relationship doesn't exist, we need only to find a reasonable ground that it does exist, which is that it should be very unlikely to find a test statistic (in the sample) of a given (large) magnitude when in fact no relationship exists in the population. If we assume that a relationship does exist, we might be guilty of not trying hard enough to prove that it doesn't exist.

5. Discuss why notations in hypotheses are usually stated in Greek letters instead of Roman letters.

Greek letters are used because hypotheses refer to relationships in the general population, not in the specific sample.

6. What is the value of chi-square when two variables are unrelated to each other? What happens to the chi-square value as variables are more closely related to each other?

When two variables are (perfectly) unrelated to each other, the value of chi-square is (exactly) zero. The value of chi-square increases as two variables are more related to each other.

7. Define chi-square mathematically. Explain the concepts of "observed" and "expected" frequencies.

Chi-square is defined as $\sum_i \frac{(O_i - E_i)^2}{E_i}$ where O_i is the observed frequency in a cell and E_i is the expected frequency in a cell. Observed frequencies are the actual counts of observations in cells. Expected frequencies are cell counts that are expected when no relationship exists between the variables.

8. What are the three test assumptions that must be satisfied in order to ensure that the chi-square test is valid?

First, the variables must be categorical. Second, the observations must be independent. Third, cells must have a minimum of five expected observations. (When the latter is not the case, it is usually because the contingency table contains a large number of rows and columns relative to the number of observations. That is, the data are spread too thinly across too many cells. To correct this problem, adjacent rows or columns are combined to create a smaller number of cells.)

9. Explain the concept of statistical significance.

The concept of statistical significance relates to the following question: On repeated sampling, *how often* would I be wrong to conclude that a relationship exists when in fact it doesn't exist? The statistical standard in the social sciences is 5 percent; that is, we are willing to tolerate a 1-in-20 chance of concluding that the null hypothesis should be rejected, when in fact it shouldn't. Standards of 1-in-100 (1 percent) are also used.

10. What is a critical value? Which two parameters determine it?

The critical value is the minimum value of a test statistic that is used to reject the null hypothesis. The critical value of any test statistic is determined by (1) the desired level of statistical significance and (2) the number of degrees of freedom (df).

11. What are the rules for determining whether a relationship is statistically significant?

We compare the absolute value of the test statistic against the critical value of the test statistic at a given level of significance. When the absolute value of the test statistic is greater than or equal to the critical value, we conclude that a relationship exists at the given level of significance. By convention, we report that relationships are not significant, are significant at the 5 percent level, or are significant at the 1 percent level. *Note:* Statistical software programs calculate the test statistic and report the level of statistical significance at which the test statistic is significant.

12. Explain how the sample size affects the level of statistical significance.

Relationships are more likely to be statistically significant when we are working with large datasets than when we are dealing with small ones. Having more information increases our confidence in our conclusions. The sample size affects the magnitude of many widely used test statistics, including chi-square.

13. What is the practical relevance of relationships? How is this different from statistical significance?

Hypothesis testing merely establishes whether a relationship is present. If a relationship is present, managers and analysts will want to describe it further in order to determine its importance for management action and public policy. This is called practical relevance (or practical significance). After the statistical significance of a relationship has been determined, analysts should ask the following questions: (1) What is the *direction* of the relationship, specifically, is it a positive or negative relationship? (2) By how *much* does one variable increase or decrease as a result of changes in the other? and (3) What is the *strength* of the relationship?

14. What is Kendall's tau-c?

Kendall's tau-c is a nonparametric alternative to chi-square. Chi-square provides no information about the direction and strength of a relationship, and it has some test assumptions, too. By contrast, Kendall's tau-c provides information about the level of significance as well as the strength and direction of relationships, and it does not have the assumption that cells must have a minimum of five expected observations. Hence, Kendall's tau-c is a useful alternative to chi-square.

15. (optional) Discuss the strategy for evaluating rival hypotheses in contingency table analysis. Also, define the terms explanation, replication, specification, and suppression. (Chapter 10 appendix)

The strategy for evaluating rival hypotheses in contingency table analysis involves taking control variables into account, discussed in the chapter appendix. Explanation is what occurs when statistically significant bivariate relationships are explained away (cease to exist) after adding the control variable. Replication is what occurs when statistically significant bivariate relationships remain significant after adding the control variable. Specification is what occurs when some statistically significant bivariate relationships are explained away after adding the control variable. Suppression is what occurs when a statistically insignificant bivariate relationship becomes significant after adding the control variable. Suppression is rare.

CRITICAL THINKING

1. Why does it make sense to test for relationships by stating the null hypothesis?

_____
_____
_____
_____
_____
_____

2. Why are standards of 1 percent and 5 percent often used? What objections might be raised against using standards of, say, .01 percent or 10 percent?

_____
_____
_____
_____
_____
_____

3. Explain why the null hypothesis is rejected when the test value exceeds or is equal to the critical value.

_____
_____
_____
_____
_____

4. **Distinguish between statistical significance and practical relevance. Can you find some examples in your area of interest in which a statistically significant result might be practically irrelevant?**

_____

_____

_____

_____

_____

_____

5. **Why must all cells in a chi-square test have a minimum of five expected observations? (See footnote 7 in Chapter 10 of the textbook.)**

_____

_____

_____

_____

_____

_____

6. **What is the critical value for a chi-square test with 13 degrees of freedom at the 1 percent level of significance? If the chi-square test statistic were 16.98, what would you conclude regarding the null hypothesis? What would you conclude if the chi-square value were 68.03?**

Critical value:

_____

_____

Conclusion if chi-square is 16.98:

_____

_____

Conclusion if chi-square is 68.03:

_____

_____

7. **A statistical software program reports a test to be significant at "$p = .035$." At what level of significance should this result be reported by the analyst (that is, 1 percent or 5 percent)? And what about "$p = .056$," "$p = .0000$," and "$p = .9989$"?**

$p = .035$:

_____

_____

$p = .056$:

_____

_____

$p = .0000$:

_____

_____

$p = .9989$:

_____

_____

8. **Formulate three null hypotheses in a study that examines the impact of community-based policing on neighborhood crime.**

Null hypothesis 1:

_____

_____

_____

Null hypothesis 2:

_____

_____

_____

Null hypothesis 3:

_____

_____

_____

9. **Use Table W10.1 to design a contingency table of overall health and the number of days worked. Make up your own data. Identify the dependent variable, and be careful where you place it in the table. Show both percentages and frequencies.**

Table W10.1 ———⌁⌁⌁— Application: Table

10. **Calculate chi-square for the hypothetical data shown in Table W10.2, and determine whether the relationship is statistically significant. Welfare outcomes (for example, time to find a job) are examined as a function of the education levels of welfare recipients. Use Table W10.3 to calculate your expected frequencies. Use Table W10.4 to calculate the chi-square values for each cell.**

Table W10.2 ———⌁⌁⌁— Welfare Outcomes by Level of Education

	Education		
Welfare outcome	No H.S. degree	H.S. degree	Some college
Low	60	55	10
Medium	35	55	15
High	25	30	20

Note: H.S. = high school.

Table W10.3 ———— ⋀⋀— Application: Welfare Outcomes by Level of Education, Expected Frequencies

Welfare outcome	Education			
	No H.S. degree	H.S. degree	Some college	Total
Low				
Medium				
High				
Total				

Note: H.S. = high school.

Table W10.4 ———— ⋀⋀— Application: Welfare Outcomes by Level of Education, Chi-Square Values

Welfare outcome	Education			
	No H.S. degree	H.S. degree	Some college	Total
Low				
Medium				
High				
Total				

Note: H.S. = high school.

11. **Examine Table W10.5. Does this contingency table satisfy the test assumptions for chi-square? Why or why not? If not, what might be done to correct the problem?**

Table W10.5 ———— ⋀⋀— Welfare Outcomes by Level of Education (Table W9.2 revised)

Welfare outcome	Education			
	No H.S. degree	H.S. degree	Some college	Total
Low	5	9	3	17
Medium	7	8	2	17
High	1	2	0	3
Total	13	19	5	37

Note: H.S. = high school.

12. **Good writing starts with knowing what to write—an outline or list of topics. Assume that you are an analyst with the National Institutes of Health, and your data show a statistically significant relationship between exercise and the risk of heart disease. Identify five things that you will want to report on in the "Results" section of your report. Consider statistical as well as practical significance. List any charts or visual aids you will use.**

1. _____

2. _____

3. _____

4. _____

5. _____

13. **Explain why Kendall's tau-c is a useful alternative to chi-square.**

_____

_____

_____

_____

_____

_____

DATA-BASED EXERCISES

Note: Some of these exercises draw on those first presented in Chapter 8.

1. **Use the Employee Attitudes dataset. Examine the relationship between stress (Stressed) and the morale of county employees (Himorale). Note the measurement scale of the variables. What do you conclude?**

   Do you consider this a causal relationship or an association? Does the analysis satisfy the assumptions of the chi-square test? If not, what categories might you combine to overcome this problem?

   _____

   _____

   _____

   _____

   _____

2. **Use the Public Perceptions dataset. Is the relationship between watching Orange TV (Watch), the county's cable television station, and trusting the county government to do what is right most of the time (Trust) statistically significant? Do you consider this a causal relationship or an association? Does the analysis satisfy the assumptions of the chi-square test? If not, how might you address this problem?**

   _____

   _____

   _____

   _____

   _____

3. **Use the Public Perceptions dataset. Examine the relationship between residents who trust the county government to do what is right most of the time (Trust) and their belief that county government works efficiently (Works). What is the practical significance of this relationship?**

   _____

   _____

   _____

   _____

   _____

4. **Use the Public Perceptions dataset. In workbook Chapter 8, Data-Based Exercise 3, you evaluated the importance of selected issues. The three most important issues were helping public schools (Pubschl), fighting illegal drug use (Figtdrug), and dealing with the problems of gangs (Gangs). Do whites and nonwhites agree on the importance of these priorities? On which issues is there a difference? Discuss the practical importance of any significant differences.**

   _____

   _____

   _____

   _____

   _____

5. **Use the Employee Attitudes dataset. This is an exercise in examining control variables. First, examine the relationship between gender (Gender) and the perceived morale of county employees (Himorale). What do you conclude? Next, test the rival hypothesis that this relationship is spuriously caused by**

stress: maybe one gender experiences a higher level of stress. (To this end, recode the variable Stressed into two groups: high stress and low stress.) What do you conclude?

_____

_____

_____

_____

_____

6. Examine the variables in the Employee Attitudes dataset. Identify five relationships that you hypothesize to be statistically significant. Test these hypotheses. What do you find?

_____

_____

_____

_____

_____

7. Compare some of the above results using chi-square and Kendall's tau-c. What do you conclude?

_____

_____

_____

_____

_____

8. In Chapter 8, Data-Based Exercise 7, you examined the relationship between attendance and academic performance based on your college experience. Now, treat those data as a sample so that you can conduct a hypothesis test. Do you find a relationship between these two variables based on the sample? Do you draw a different conclusion from the one you drew in Chapter 8? If yes, why is it different?

_____

_____

_____

_____

_____

FURTHER READING

There exists no shortage of "general purpose" introductory statistics texts, and most of them discuss hypothesis testing. If you seek additional assistance on this topic, we suggest that you peruse your local library shelves until you find a book that you like. Statistics books explain this topic in similar yet subtly different ways. The textbooks suggested here explain hypothesis testing and contingency table analysis in a clear manner. We hope that you like our approach, but feel free to choose whatever works for you. Sometimes, it is just a matter of seeing the same thing from different angles.

Some statistics texts have been mentioned in Chapters 6 and 7, and these will likely help here, too. Sam Kash Kachigan, *Multivariate Statistical Analysis: A Conceptual Introduction,* 2nd ed. (New York: Radius Press, 1991) is an inexpensive book that does an exemplary job of explaining advanced statistics concepts in nonmathematical terms, but the coverage of topics is advanced, perhaps aimed at doctoral students. Another option is Tari Renner, *Statistics Unraveled: A Practical Guide to Using Data in Decision Making* (Washington, D.C.: International City/County Management Association, 1988). Of course, you can also compare our treatment with that of another book in public affairs, Kenneth Meyer, Jeffrey Brudney, and John Bohte, *Applied Statistics for Public Administration,* 8th ed. (Florence, Ky.: Wadsworth), 2011.

CHAPTER

11

Measures of Association

Q & A

1. *What is proportional reduction in error?*

Proportional reduction in error (PRE) is the improvement, expressed as a fraction, in predicting a dependent variable from knowledge of the independent variable. PRE ratios range from 0.00 (no association or improvement in prediction) to 1.00 (perfect association or prediction). Although there are no absolute standards for PRE scores, many analysts regard scores of less than 0.25 as indicating a weak association, scores between 0.25 and 0.50, a moderate association, and scores above 0.50, a strong association.

2. *What are paired cases?*

Some PRE statistics are calculated based on paired cases. Similar pairs are pairs of observations that have similar rankings on two variables, that is, observations rank similarly low (or high) on both variables. Dissimilar pairs are pairs of observations that have reverse ranking on two variables—one observation scores high and the other low, and vice versa, on both variables. Tied pairs are those that have similar rankings on one variable and dissimilar rankings on the other variable. PRE statistics based on paired cases have a range of –1 to +1, which provides information about both the strength and the direction of relationships. For example, a PRE test statistic based on paired cases with a value of –0.57 indicates a strong, negative relationship between two variables.

3. *What does the term dependent samples refer to?*

Dependent samples (also called related samples) are those in which the selection of one subject in a sample affects the selection of subjects in another group. Examples of dependent samples are those that involve before-and-after test scores, subjects that have been matched (or paired) in some way, and evaluators' ratings. Separate statistical tests exist for dependent samples.

4. *What is the difference between symmetric and directional measures?*

Some PRE measures vary depending on which variable is designated as dependent. Such measures are called directional. By contrast, symmetric measures do not vary according to which variable is designated as dependent.

5. *Name four measures of association for two ordinal variables, and compare them.*

Four measures of association for two ordinal variables are gamma (γ), Somer's d, Kendall's tau-b (τ_b) and Kendall's tau-c (τ_c). These PRE statistics differ chiefly in the manner in which ties are taken into account. Of these, tau-c often has the smallest PRE value and is widely used.

6. For what purpose is Goodman and Kruskal's tau used?

Goodman and Kruskal's tau is a PRE measure that is used for testing the association of two nominal variables.

7. What is the goodness-of-fit test?

The goodness-of-fit test is used to determine whether an ordinal distribution or test result is consistent with a predetermined norm.

8. For what purpose is the McNemar test used? How does it differ from other tests?

The McNemar test is used for two-by-two tables with paired observations. It is frequently used for testing discrimination. The McNemar test differs from many other tests in that it determines the level at which *dissimilar outcomes* are statistically significant. The McNemar test ignores cases with similar outcomes.

9. What problems are associated with small samples, and how are they addressed by two-by-two tables? What are some tests for small samples?

Tests often fail to reject the null hypothesis when samples are small. Analysts frequently combine categories in order to increase the information in each cell, thus reducing the number of rows and columns. This may result in two-by-two tables. The chi-square with continuity correction and the Fisher exact test are tests for small samples.

10. Which test statistics are used for comparing ratings across programs or program components?

Kruskal-Wallis' H and the Friedman test are often used to compare ratings across programs or program components. Both tests assign ranks to raters' ratings and then determine the level at which the mean of ranks is different across each of the different programs or program components.

11. How does the Friedman test differ from the Kruskal-Wallis' H test?

Whereas the Kruskal-Wallis' H test assumes independent observations, the Friedman test assumes dependent observations.

CRITICAL THINKING

1. Explain why PRE is a measure of the strength of relationships.

_____

_____

_____

_____

_____

_____

2. Give some examples of dependent and independent samples.

_____

_____

_____

_____

_____

_____

3. In what ways is tau-c a more useful measure than chi-square?

_____

_____

_____

_____

_____

_____

4. You have conducted a citizen survey and want to know whether respondents' assessments about environmental and economic conditions are associated. Both items are measured on a seven-point Likert scale. Which test statistic might you use, and why?

Test statistic and rationale:

_____

_____

_____

_____

_____

_____

5. You are a senior staff member with the Federal Aviation Administration. Flight delays have been a major issue with the public of late, and one of your contractors has proposed a new system that promises to reduce the number of delays that exceed 10 minutes. To test whether the system works, you will implement it at a major airport and measure delays during the late afternoon rush hour.

   The average delay will be calculated daily for the late afternoon period. Which test statistic can be used to answer the question of whether the new system has reduced average delays that are greater than 10 minutes? For this purpose, use a dichotomous variable that measures, for each day, whether the average delay exceeded 10 minutes. Also, what is the fewest number of days that the airport must implement the system in order to determine (at the 1 percent level of significance) whether the system effectively reduces the average delay to less than 10 minutes?

Test statistic and rationale:

_____

_____

_____

Minimum sample size:

_____

_____

_____

6. You are a manager with a state employment agency. In one of your districts, managers have implemented a new program, and after six months of trial (and error), it is decided to bring in a panel of outside experts to evaluate it. You would like to have the option to later disregard any evaluator whose assessment sharply disagrees with others. How many experts should you bring in? How many different aspects should they each evaluate? Should they evaluate the same aspects or different aspects? Which statistical test should you use, and how does that affect your answer?

Number of evaluators and rationale:

_____

_____

_____

Test statistic and number of items:

_____
_____
_____

7. **As a manager, you want to know whether your employees are treating service requests from white and minority program clients in a similar manner. You decide to send pairs of white and minority testers to your agencies with similar service requests. Which test statistic might you use, and why?**

_____
_____
_____
_____
_____
_____

8. **If you wanted to examine the effects of different job training programs on employment outcomes, which statistical test would you use, and why? (*Note:* Answers vary depending on the level of measurement you choose with regard to these variables.)**

_____
_____
_____
_____
_____
_____

9. **Identify questions that can be addressed using the following tests: McNemar test, chi-square, and Kendall's tau-c. Identify one question per test.**

McNemar:

_____
_____
_____

Chi-square:

_____
_____
_____

Kendall's tau-c:

_____
_____
_____

DATA-BASED EXERCISES

1. **Use the Public Perceptions dataset. In Chapter 10 of this workbook, you used chi-square to examine the relationship between residents who trust the county government to do what is right most of the**

time (Trust) and their belief that county government works efficiently (Works). Reexamine this relationship using measures of gamma, Somer's d, Kendall's tau-b, and Kendall's tau-c. What do you conclude?

_____
_____
_____
_____
_____

2. Use the Public Perceptions dataset. What is the association between having a positive view of the county government (Posview) and satisfaction with the various services that are mentioned, such as law enforcement (Lawenf)?

_____
_____
_____
_____
_____

3. Three interviewers are evaluating five job candidates. After interviews and analysis of qualifications and skills, the interviewers are asked to rank the five job candidates. The rankings shown in Table W11.1 are obtained (1 = high, 5 = low). Which job candidate has the highest level of approval? Do the raters agree? How do your results change when a fourth evaluator is added with rankings identical to those of the first evaluator?

_____
_____
_____
_____
_____

Table W11.1 —~~— Ranking of Job Candidates

| | Job candidates | | | | |
Interviewer	#1	#2	#3	#4	#5
1	2	1	4	3	5
2	4	2	3	1	5
3	3	2	1	4	5

4. A manager wants to know whether whites and minorities are receiving similar or disparate answers to their inquiries. To this end, 15 pairs of testers are sent with identical questions. Testers report to the study supervisor the answers as received, which are then evaluated as satisfactory or unsatisfactory. The result shown in Table W11.2 is obtained. Do whites and minorities receive different treatment?

_____
_____
_____
_____

Table W11.2 ⎯⎯⎯〰⎯⎯ Outcomes by Race

| | White | | |
Minority	Satisfactory	Unsatisfactory	Total
Satisfactory	8	1	9
Unsatisfactory	3	3	6
Total	11	4	15

5. In a sample of 57 students, 35 pass a test. Is this result consistent with a norm that states that at least 67 percent of students should pass the test? Is it consistent with a norm of 80 percent? What test statistics should you use?

_____

_____

_____

_____

_____

6. Examine the Employee Attitudes dataset. Use Kendall's tau-c to test five associations of your choice. Of those that are statistically significant, which are also practically relevant? Why? Practice writing up your results.

_____

_____

_____

_____

_____

FURTHER READING

Many basic statistics books have separate chapters on the use of the statistics for categorical variables. Comprehensive treatment of this subject is found in Lawrence L. Giventer, *Statistical Analysis for Public Administration,* 2nd ed. (Burlington, Mass.: Jones & Bartlett, 2007). This book covers the material presented in this single chapter over multiple chapters, and numerous applications and examples of hand calculations of test formulas are provided.

The T-Test

Q & A

1. When should a t-test be used?

T-tests are used for testing whether two groups have different means. One variable is dichotomous, whereas the other is continuous.

2. What is the null hypothesis of a t-test?

The null hypothesis of a t-test is that the means of a variable do not differ between two groups in the population; that is, the two means are equal. Rejecting the null hypothesis implies that the two group means are different in the population.

3. Name four t-test assumptions.

(1) One variable is continuous, and the other variable is dichotomous.
(2) The two distributions have equal variances.
(3) Observations are independent.
(4) The two distributions are normally distributed.

4. How do researchers test for the normality of variables?

Researchers typically use a combination of visual inspection and statistical tests, such as the Kolmogorov-Smirnov test, to determine the normality of variables. It is acceptable to consider variables as being normally distributed when they visually appear to be so, even when the null hypothesis of normality is rejected by normality tests. Of course, variables are preferred that are supported by both visual inspection and normality tests.

5. What is the purpose of the Levene's test of the equality of variances?

The purpose of the Levene's test is to test whether groups have equal variances. This test is used to test one of the four t-test assumptions and is always used prior to testing the equality of means.

6. What is a paired t-test?

The paired t-test often is used when using before-and-after measurements, such as when assessing student scores before and after tests. Paired t-tests are used when analysts have a dependent rather than an independent sample.

7. What is a one-sample t-test?

A one-sample t-test is used to test whether the mean of a variable is significantly different from a user-specified value.

8. *What is the difference between parametric and nonparametric tests? Which type of test is the t-test?*

Parametric tests make assumptions about the distribution of data and also are used to make inferences about population parameters. Formally, the term *parametric* means that a test makes assumptions about the distribution of the underlying population. Parametric tests have more test assumptions than nonparametric tests, and most typically assume that the variable is continuous and normally distributed.

9. *What are the advantages and disadvantages of using nonparametric alternatives to t-tests?*

The chief advantage of nonparametric alternatives is that they do not require that continuous variables be normally distributed. The chief disadvantage of nonparametric alternatives is that they are less likely to reject the null hypothesis. A further, minor disadvantage is that nonparametric alternatives do not provide descriptive information about variable means; separate analysis is required for that.

10. *What is a nonparametric alternative to the independent-samples t-test?*

Nonparametric alternatives to the independent-samples test are the Mann-Whitney (U) and Wilcoxon (W) tests. The Mann-Whitney and Wilcoxon tests are equivalent, and both are simplifications of the more general Kruskal-Wallis' H test, discussed in Chapter 11.

11. *What is a nonparametric alternative to the paired-samples t-test?*

A nonparametric alternative to the paired-samples t-test is the Wilcoxon signed rank test.

12. *What is a nonparametric alternative to the one-sample t-test?*

The Wilcoxon signed rank test can also be adapted as a nonparametric alternative to the one-sample t-test. Then, analysts create a second variable that, for each observation, is the test value.

CRITICAL THINKING

1. Explain the importance of the four test assumptions of the independent-samples t-test.

_____
_____
_____
_____
_____
_____

2. Why is the assumption of equal variances irrelevant for the paired-samples t-test?

_____
_____
_____
_____
_____
_____

3. Explain the following statement regarding tests for normality: "Whereas failure to reject the null hypothesis indicates normal distribution of a variable, rejecting the null hypothesis does not indicate that the variable is not normally distributed."

_____
_____
_____
_____
_____
_____

4. Table W12.1 is the printout of a t-test (independent samples). The continuous variable is an index variable of environmental concern. The dichotomous variable is a measure of education (college versus no college). Interpret and write up the results. What other information would you like to have about this relationship?

_____

_____

_____

_____

_____

_____

Table W12.1 ⎯⎯⎯⎯⎯⎯ Analysis of Environmental Concerns by Education: T-Test Output

Variable	Levene's test for equality of variances			T-test for the equality of means		
	F	*p*		*t*	*df*	*p* (2–tailed)
Environmental concern	1.065	.304	Equal variances assumed	3.705	118.00	.000
			Equal variances not assumed	3.728	117.92	.000

5. Table W12.2 is the printout of a paired-samples t-test. The data are before-and-after measurements of a public safety program. Interpret and write up the results. What other information would you like to have about this relationship?

_____

_____

_____

_____

_____

_____

Table W12.2 ⎯⎯⎯⎯⎯⎯ Comparing "Before" and "After" Results of a Public Safety Program: Paired T-Test Printout

Pair	Mean	T-test for the equality of means		
		t	*df*	*p* (2–tailed)
Before - After	−1.497	7.310	193	.000

6. Table W12.3 shows the result of the Kolmogorov-Smirnov test for a variable and three of its transformations. Which variable(s) should the analysts consider for subsequent use?

_____

_____

_____

_____

_____

_____

Table W12.3 ——— ⌇⌇⌇— Testing for Normality

	Kolmogorov-Smirnov		
	Statistic	df	Significance
Index	0.095	102	0.025
SQRT index	0.304	102	0.200
Log index	0.098	102	0.006
Squared index	0.057	102	0.200

7. You are analyzing your data and, using a boxplot, you see some outliers. Should your initial approach be to remove them or to keep them? Why? What are the pros and cons of each approach?

_____

_____

_____

_____

_____

_____

DATA-BASED EXERCISES

1. Use the Watershed dataset. Replicate the analysis in the text. First, analyze the normality of the variable Conpolut and consider various transformations, as shown in Figures 12.3 and 12.4 of the textbook. Then, replicate the t-test for comparing the East (defined as Northeast and Southeast combined) with all other regions.

_____

_____

_____

_____

_____

2. Use the Watershed dataset. Do states in the East vary in the number of fish and wildlife advisories that have been made? (Use the variable Advisory.) Is the variable Advisory normally distributed? If not, what transformation do you suggest?

_____

_____

_____

_____

_____

3. Use the Public Perceptions dataset. An analyst wants to know whether men and women have different perceptions of customer service. To this end, we will use an index variable of customer satisfaction (see Chapter 3); the index variable is provided on the dataset as the last variable, Satisfac, but you can also practice making this index variable in the following way:

From among those respondents who have had contact with a county employee (that is, if contact = 1), create an index variable of "customer service" that is composed of the six survey items: "employees were helpful," "employees treated me with courtesy and respect," "employees were friendly," "service was provided without mistakes," "the service experience exceeded my expectations," and "service was provided in a timely manner." If you are using SPSS, see Chapter 20 of this workbook for instructions on creating index variables in SPSS. After you have either created this variable or identified this variable in the dataset, address the question of whether men and women vary in their customer satisfaction experience.

_____

_____

_____

_____

_____

4. Use the Public Perceptions dataset. An analyst wants to know whether the index variable of customer service varies across race. Recode the Ethnic variable to distinguish among whites, blacks, other races, and Hispanics. If you are using SPSS, see Chapter 20 of this workbook for instructions on recoding variables in SPSS.

_____

_____

_____

_____

_____

5. Men and women are asked to rank six issues in the order of priority. See Table W12.4. Do men and women differ in their order of priorities? Which test statistic would you use? Can you think of some other situations that match this scenario?

Table W12.4 ⎯⎯⎯⎯⎯ ∿∿ Rank Ordering of Six Priorities

Men	Women
1	3
2	1
3	2
4	6
5	4
6	5

6. A group of 12 welfare recipients participate in training. Before-and-after abilities are measured through a standardized test. See Table W12.5. Is there evidence of improvement? Compare the results of both the paired-samples t-test and the nonparametric alternative.

_____

_____

_____

_____

_____

Table W12.5 ──────〜〜〜── Before-and-After Test Scores

Recipient	Before	After
1	4.5	6.7
2	3.2	4.2
3	5.8	5.2
4	3.9	4.3
5	4.2	4.1
6	3.9	4.8
7	2.6	3.2
8	5.2	4.8
9	4.5	4.5
10	3.9	4.1
11	3.8	3.6
12	4.2	5.9

7. Consider Table W12.5 again. Is the after-test score consistent with a norm of 5.0? With a norm of 6.0? Use both parametric and nonparametric tests. Compare the results.

_____

_____

_____

_____

_____

8. T-tests can be used in performance analysis and evaluation. The psychosocial functional score (PFS) is used to assess school-aged children's psychosocial behaviors. A score of 25 points or above is considered normal. A school counseling program has used the PFS to assess participating students' progress. A sample of 15 participating students is tested, and their PFS scores are 29, 32, 18, 23, 27, 19, 34, 32, 27, 27, 23, 26, 32, 29, and 34. Conduct a performance evaluation to assess if the participants' average PFS score is greater than 25. Write a summary to report your findings to the program manager, who knows nothing about statistics.

_____

_____

_____

_____

_____

FURTHER READING

Most statistics books discuss t-tests, although they vary in their coverage of formulas and test assumptions. An in-depth discussion of t-tests is found in David Howell, *Statistical Methods for Psychology,* 7th ed. (Belmont, Calif.: Wadsworth, 2009), chap. 7. The *SPSS User's Guide* (Chicago: SPSS, Inc.) has excellent examples of the use of t-tests in practice and, in a separate chapter, gives some further examples of variable transformations. Another solid treatment is found in Ronet Bachman and Raymond Paternoster, *Statistical Methods for Criminology and Criminal Justice,* 3rd ed. (New York: McGraw-Hill, 2008).

CHAPTER

13

Analysis of Variance (ANOVA)

Q & A

1. For what purpose is ANOVA used?

ANOVA is used for testing whether three or more groups have different means and, if so, which groups have different means. By comparison, t-tests are used for testing whether two groups have different means.

2. What is the purpose of the global F-test in ANOVA?

The ANOVA global F-test tests for differences among any of the means.

3. What are the four test assumptions for ANOVA?

(1) One variable is continuous, and the other variable is ordinal or nominal.
(2) The group distributions have equal variances.
(3) Observations are independent.
(4) The variable is normally distributed in each of the groups.

4. What is a post-hoc test? Name three post-hoc tests.

Post-hoc tests are tests that test all possible group differences and do so in a manner that maintains a true (5 percent or 1 percent) level of significance. Three popular post-hoc tests are Tukey, Bonferroni, and Scheffe. The Scheffe test is the most conservative, the Tukey test is best when many comparisons are made (that is, there are many groups), and the Bonferroni test is preferred when few comparisons are made.

5. What are homogenous subsets?

Homogeneous subsets are groups with insignificant differences of their means.

6. How can ANOVA test the linearity of relationships that involve a continuous variable and an ordinal variable?

ANOVA can also be used to test the linearity of interval-ordinal relationships, that is, whether the change in means follows a linear, an increasing, or a decreasing pattern according to the ordering of the ordinal variable. The appropriate F-test is the statistic reported as the "linear term for unweighted sum of squares" in ANOVA tables.

7. What is MANOVA? How is it different from two-way ANOVA?

MANOVA is a technique for analyzing the effects of multiple independent variables on multiple dependent variables. Two-way ANOVA is a technique for analyzing the effects of two independent variables on one dependent variable.

8. *What is the Kruskal-Wallis H test?*

The Kruskal-Wallis H test is a nonparametric alternative to one-way ANOVA. As a nonparametric method, the Kruskal-Wallis H test does not assume normal populations, but the test does assume similarly shaped distributions for each group. A limitation of this nonparametric test is that it does not provide group means, post-hoc tests, or analysis of which groups are homogenous.

CRITICAL THINKING

1. Your data include a measure of air pollution that is measured on a continuous scale, as well as another variable that measures the location of that air pollution in five counties. Which test statistic should you use to examine whether mean pollution levels vary across counties?

_____

_____

_____

_____

_____

_____

2. Table W13.1 is a sample output ANOVA table, comparing educational outcomes across five different groups of students. Interpret the output.

_____

_____

_____

_____

_____

_____

Table W13.1 ⎯⎯⎯⎯⎯⎯ ANOVA Table

	Sum of squares	df	Mean square	F-test	p
Between groups	2415.2	5	490.2	3.538	.006
Within groups	13579.8	98	138.6		
Total	16031.0	103			

3. ANOVA can be useful, even outside your field of work. Conduct the following experiment. Choose one of your favorite locations away from your home. It could be a supermarket, a shopping mall, or a playground. Identify at least three routes to get there. Now, choose the route you use most often. Record your travel time to that location (in minutes) up to 10 times. Then, choose an alternative route and record your travel time (in minutes) up to 10 times. Choose a third route and record your travel time up to 10 times. In this experiment, make sure you use the same mode of transportation (for example, car, bike, or public transit) each time and obtain your measurements at approximately the same time of day to rule out the impact of these confounding variables on travel time. Compare travel times for each route to determine whether the mean travel times differ between routes. Is the route you use most often the fastest?

_____

_____

_____

_____

_____

_____

4. In the preceding exercise, the dependent variable is travel time. You tested the impact of various routes (the independent variable) on travel time. Because these routes are unrelated to each other, you tested the mean differences of three independent samples. You can follow the same logic to test the impact of times of day on travel time. For example, you could record your travel times at 10:00 am, 2:00 pm, and 7:00 pm up to 10 times each to determine whether there is any mean difference in travel time at different times of a day. You could use the same method to test your travel times to work. If you have a flexible schedule that allows you to be at work at the time of your choice, you could use this method to choose the least time-consuming and most energy-saving way to get to work. This would truly be a performance improvement for you and for your organization. Can you think of any other ways to use ANOVA to improve your work performance or your life?

_____

_____

_____

_____

_____

_____

5. Table W13.2 is a sample output ANOVA table with linearity test. Interpret the output.

_____

_____

_____

_____

_____

_____

Table W13.2 ⎯⎯⎯⎯ ∿∿ ⎯ ANOVA Table with Linearity Test

			Sum of squares	df	Variance (s^2)	F-test	p
Between groups	Combined		12.041	3	4.014	2.797	.043
	Linear term	Unweighted	7.701	1	7.701	5.367	.022
		Weighted	7.482	1	7.482	5.215	.024
		Deviation	4.558	2	2.279	1.588	.209
Within groups			162.137	113	1.435		
Total			174.178	116			

6. An analyst conducts a test of homogeneity of variances in ANOVA and finds that the Levene's statistic = .911, p = .461 > .05. What does the analyst conclude?

_____

_____

_____

_____

_____

_____

7. Table W13.3 is a sample output two-way ANOVA table. Interpret the output.

_____

_____

_____

_____

_____

_____

Table W13.3 ⎯⎯⎯⎯ ⟋⋀⋀⟍ ⎯ Two-Way ANOVA Table

Source	Sum of squares	df	Mean square	F-test	p
Model	1642.8	24	68.44	4.507	.000
Var A	229.8	4	57.45	3.783	.007
Var B	85.5	5	17.11	1.127	.351
Var A * Var B	409.5	14	29.25	1.926	.032
Error	1488.2	98	15.19		
Total	3130.9	122			

DATA-BASED EXERCISES

1. ANOVA is a useful tool in performance comparisons. A nonprofit foundation funds a program to reduce accidents among school-aged children. The employees in the program conduct regular education workshops for students and teachers. The daily number of accidents per 1,000 students is used to assess the performance of the program in reducing accidents among students. The program is operated in school A, which collected the following data on 10 randomly selected days: 3.82, 1.01, 5.96, 8.99, 8.85, 5.54, 0.14, 4.07, 7.65, and 1.39. You are a performance analyst whose job it is to assess the performance of this program in school A. To conduct your evaluation, you collect data from two schools (school B and school C) that do not have these programs (that is, the control groups). The following data are for school B: 6.58, 0.59, 7.00, 7.17, 7.83, 8.68, 1.17, 5.50, 6.84, and 4.09. For school C the data are as follows: 9.47, 4.86, 8.65, 5.54, 6.45, 2.71, 8.63, 9.30, 7.37, and 7.09. Assume normal distributions of the data in each group and determine whether the program in school A has a lower number of accidents.

_____

_____

_____

_____

_____

_____

2. Use the Public Perceptions dataset. An analyst wants to know whether the index variable of customer service varies across race. Recode the variable Ethnic to distinguish among whites, blacks, other races, and Hispanics, and then calculate the means for each of these groups. Then use ANOVA to determine whether any of these differences are statistically significant.

_____

_____

_____

_____

_____

_____

3. Use the Public Perceptions dataset. An analyst wants to know whether incomes vary by age groups. Treat the income variable as a continuous variable, and treat the age variable as an ordinal variable. Calculate the means for each of these groups, and then use ANOVA to determine whether any of these differences are statistically significant. For which age groups is the relationship linear?

_____

_____

_____

_____

_____

_____

4. Use the Watershed dataset. An analyst wants to know whether the level of conventional pollutants (conpolut) is associated with the number of aquatic/wetland species at risk (speatrsk). What are your conclusions?

_____

_____

_____

_____

_____

_____

FURTHER READING

Numerous books discuss ANOVA. See Sam Kash Kachigan, *Multivariate Statistical Analysis: A Conceptual Introduction,* 2nd ed. (New York: Radius Press, 1991); Chapter 5 provides a most lucent discussion of ANOVA. The *SPSS Base Applications Guide* has an excellent, practical discussion and carries this topic further. Analysts in health care settings will want a more detailed discussion, such as in Barbara Tabachnick and Linda Fidell, *Using Multivariate Statistics,* 5th ed. (New York: HarperCollins, 2006), or M. Kutner, et al., *Applied Linear Statistical Models* (New York: McGraw-Hill, 2004).

CHAPTER

14

Simple Regression

Q & A

1. For what purpose is simple regression used?

Simple regression is used for testing the relationship between two continuous variables, whereby one variable is the dependent variable and the other is the independent variable.

2. How is simple regression used for testing hypotheses? What test statistic is used, and how is it defined?

Simple regression involves estimating the relationship between variables through a straight line (regression line), $y = a + bx$, where a is the intercept (or constant), and b is the slope. The slope is also called the regression coefficient. If the slope is statistically different from zero, then a relationship is said to exist between the variables in the population. To determine whether the slope equals zero, a t-test is performed. The test statistic is defined as the slope (b) divided by the standard error of the slope (se[b]).

3. What is the interpretation of the coefficient of determination, R-square (R^2), and what values can it assume?

R-square can assume values between 0 and +1. The value of R-square is interpreted as the percentage of variation in the dependent variable that is explained by the independent variable.

4. Why is linearity important in regression analysis?

Regression analysis estimates the relationship between variables as a straight line over the *entire range* of observations. If the pattern is curved (for example, parabolic) or broken (for example, upward sloping for one part of the observations and downward sloping for the rest), the assumption of linearity is violated, and the statistical significance of regression coefficients will be underestimated.

5. What is the difference between the observed and predicted values of the dependent variable? What is the error term?

The predicted value of y (defined, based on the regression model, as $y = a + bx$) is typically different from the actual observed value of y. The predicted value of the dependent variable y is sometimes indicated as $\hat{y}$ (pronounced "y-hat"). The difference between y and $\hat{y}$ is called the regression error or error term (e). Hence, $y = \hat{y} + e$.

6. What is Pearson's correlation coefficient, r? What values can it assume, and how is it interpreted?

Pearson's correlation coefficient, r, measures the association between two continuous variables. It does not distinguish between a dependent and an independent variable, as does simple regression. Pearson's correlation coefficient ranges from -1 to $+1$. The sign indicates the direction of the relationship, which is the same sign as the slope coefficient. Values of r^2 between 0.0 and 0.20 indicate weak associations, values between 0.20 and 0.40 indicate moderate associations, values between 0.40 and 0.65 indicate strong associations, and values above 0.65 are considered to indicate very strong associations. For the two-variable, simple regression model, $r^2 = R^2$.

7. How is the Pearson's correlation coefficient, r, different from the slope (regression coefficient), b?

Comparison of the measures r and b (the slope) sometimes causes confusion. Pearson's correlation coefficient, r, indicates not the regression slope but rather the extent to which observations lie close to it. A steep regression line (large b) can have observations that lie either loosely or closely scattered around it, as can a shallow (more horizontal) regression line.

8. What purpose does Spearman's rank order correlation coefficient (ρ) serve?

Spearman's rank order correlation coefficient, ρ, is a nonparametric alternative to simple regression and Pearson's correlation coefficient, r. Spearman's rank order correlation coefficient looks at correlation among the ranks of the data rather than among the values. Because Spearman's rank correlation coefficient examines correlation among the ranks of variables, it can also be used with ordinal-level data. Spearman's rank correlation coefficient has a "percent variation explained" interpretation, similar to the other measures described here.

CRITICAL THINKING

1. Explain why variables are assumed to be linearly related in simple regression.

_____

_____

_____

_____

_____

_____

2. Explain why the slope can be used as a test of the relationship of two variables in simple regression.

_____

_____

_____

_____

_____

_____

3. Explain why, if b is statistically significant, then r should be statistically significant, too.

_____

_____

_____

_____

_____

_____

4. Draw a scatterplot between two variables that has a large r^2 and a small, negative b. Then, draw another scatterplot that has a small r^2 and a large, positive b. Show the regression lines in each.

5. You are a program manager for a welfare agency and want to know if a relationship exists between the length of time that people receive welfare (in months) and their education (total years). Both variables are continuous. Table W14.1 is the hypothetical output from your simple regression model. Interpret the results.

_____

_____

_____

_____

_____

_____

Table W14.1 ─────〰〰── Simple Regression Output

R	R-square	SEE
0.002	0.000	1.125

Dependent variable: Unemployment duration

Coefficients

Model	Unstandardized coefficients		t	Sig.
	b	SE		
Constant	0.6710	0.034	19.63	0.000
Education	0.0015	0.033	0.045	0.965

Note: SE = standard error; Sig. = significance.

6. Explain how Spearman's rank coefficient transforms interval-level values into ranks. Then explain why the Spearman's rank coefficient can also be used with ordinal-level variables.

_____

_____

_____

_____

_____

_____

DATA-BASED EXERCISES

1. Use the Productivity dataset. Examine the bivariate relationship between having authority (Jobauthr) and knowledge (Jobknowl) to do one's job. Use simple regression. What are your findings?

_____

_____

_____

_____

_____

2. Use the Productivity dataset. Examine the bivariate relationship between employees' perception of productivity (Productivity) and the perceptions of having adequate authority to do one's job (Jobauthr). Use both simple regression and Pearson's correlation coefficient.

_____

_____

_____

_____

_____

3. Examine the normality of variables used in the preceding exercises (see Chapter 12). Are Jobauthr, Productivity, and Jobknowl normally distributed? On what basis do you reach this conclusion? Is there any transformation that can make them normal?

_____

_____

_____

_____

_____

4. Use the Community Indicators dataset. Which variables are associated with median household incomes?

_____

_____

_____

_____

_____

5. Use the Community Indicators dataset. Create the variables "Cancers per capita" and "Rapes per capita." Which variables are associated with these variables?

_____

_____

_____

_____

_____

6. Use the Productivity dataset. Compare employees' perceptions of productivity (Productivity) with those of the outside consultant (Wkctrpro). What test statistic might you use for this comparison?

_____

_____

_____

_____

_____

7. Regression is a useful tool in performance analysis. Choose a variable that you think influences your academic performance. (Many students would say that effort, attendance, instruction quality, level of difficulty, and study methods are keys to improving academic performance—choose one.) Create a database that includes all the courses you have taken in college. Recall your experiences and performance (for example, your grade) in those courses. For example, you could measure effort with the number of hours spent studying for the course weekly. Level of difficulty could be measured with "very difficult," "difficult," or "not difficult." Use simple regression to analyze the relationship between the variable of your choice and your academic performance. What do you conclude? Write a report that summarizes your findings for a person who knows nothing about statistics.

_____

_____

_____

_____

_____

FURTHER READING

Many books mentioned in the previous chapters also discuss simple regression and the other statistics described here. By now you may have found one or two other statistics texts that are useful to you, and these are likely to discuss these statistics, as well. In Chapter 15, we identify some further readings for multiple regression, and these books typically also discuss simple regression.

Multiple Regression

Q & A

1. For what purpose is multiple regression used?

Multiple regression is used to examine the effect of control variables on the relationship between one dependent variable and one (or more) independent variables.

2. What is full model specification? How does full model specification relate to a nomothetic mode of explanation?

Full model specification means that analysts attempt to identify *all the variables* that affect a dependent variable. Fully specified models have two parts: (1) the identification of *the most important factors* that affect a dependent variable (these are independent variables) and (2) the identification of *all other factors* that affect the dependent variable, whose cumulative effects are contained in the error term. The identification of the most important factors is called a nomothetic mode of explanation.

3. What key assumption is made about the error term in regression? How is this assumption examined?

The error term is interpreted as the effect on y of all other influences on y that are *not included* as independent variables in the regression model. A key assumption is that the cumulative effect of these independent variables on the regression is zero. Examination of this assumption is based on plots of the standardized residuals against the standardized predicted variable. When the cumulative effect of the error term is zero, its pattern is randomly distributed around (0,0) of the error term plot.

4. How many independent variables are commonly identified in multiple regression? What is the relationship among independent variables?

Multiple regression models typically have five to seven independent variables, although some have many more. Independent variables should be the most important factors that affect the dependent variable. Correlations among independent variables should be low.

5. What is the interpretation of regression coefficients in multiple regression?

In multiple regression, the regression coefficients are interpreted as their effect on the dependent variable, controlled for the effect of all other independent variables included in the regression.

6. What undesirable property does the coefficient of determination, R-square (R^2), have in multiple regression, and how is this problem overcome?

R-square is interpreted as the percentage of variation in the dependent variable that is explained by the independent variable(s). R-square has the undesirable property that it increases with the number of independent variables included in the regression model. Adjusted R-square ($\bar{R}^2$) controls for the number of independent variables in the regression and is always equal to or less than R-square.

7. What are standardized coefficients (beta values)? Why are they used?

Beta values (or betas) are standardized regression coefficients. Beta (β) is defined as the change produced in the dependent variable by a unit of change in the independent variable when both are measured in terms of standard deviation units. Betas are unitless, allowing analysts to compare the impact of different independent variables on the dependent variable. It is appropriate to compare betas across independent variables in the same regression model but not across different models.

8. What is the function of the global F-test in multiple regression?

The global F-test examines the overall effect of all independent variables jointly on the dependent variable. The null hypothesis is that the overall effect of all independent variables jointly on the dependent variables is statistically insignificant. The alternate hypothesis is that this overall effect is statistically significant. The null hypothesis implies that none of the regression coefficients is statistically significant, that is, $b_1 = b_2 = \ldots = 0$; the alternate hypothesis implies that at least one of the regression coefficients is statistically significant.

9. What are dummy variables? Why are they useful? Give an example of the use of dummy variables.

Dummy variables allow researchers to use nominal-level variables in multiple regression. Dummy variables are variables that have values of either one or zero. See Table 15.2 in the textbook for an example of recoding. The number of dummy variables equals the number of measurement categories *minus one*.

10. Why are regression assumptions so important?

When the assumptions of multiple regression are violated, the results of multiple regression may be invalid.

11. Name six assumptions of multiple regression.

(1) No observation is an outlier.
(2) No multicollinearity is present among the independent variables.
(3) The relationships between the independent variables and the dependent variable are linear.
(4) The error term is homoscedastic across the range of each independent variable.
(5) Error terms are not serially correlated (or autocorrelated).
(6) Variables are measured and specified accurately.

12. Explain the concept of outliers and how they may affect the results of multiple regression. Also, explain how outliers are detected and how the problem of outliers is remedied.

Outliers are observations with unusual values that may affect the statistical significance of regression coefficients, notably by influencing the regression slope. Outliers are detected by the size of their error term. Specifically, they are observations whose error terms either exceed +3 standard deviations or are less than –3 standard deviations. The problem of outliers usually is remedied by excluding such observations from analysis.

13. Explain the concept of multicollinearity and how it affects the results of multiple regression. Also, explain how multicollinearity is detected and how the problem of multicollinearity is remedied.

Multicollinearity is the problem of two or more independent variables that are so highly correlated that their individual effects on the dependent variable are statistically indistinguishable. Multicollinearity affects the results of multiple regression by causing the regression coefficients of multicollinear variables to be insignificant. Multicollinearity is usually first suspected when regression coefficients are insignificant, even though in bivariate analysis they are known to be highly significant. Multicollinearity is detected formally by variance inflation factor (VIF) scores that exceed 5 or 10. Multicollinearity is remedied by combining substantively related variables into a single index variable, by dropping a collinear variable, or by replacing one variable by a substantively similar but empirically dissimilar variable.

14. *Explain the importance of linearity. How is curvilinearity detected, and how is it remedied?*

Multiple regression assumes that independent variables are *linearly* correlated with the dependent variable. When relationships are nonlinear (such as being curvilinear), regression coefficients underestimate the significance of the relationship. In some instances, the regression coefficient will be estimated as being insignificant when it is not. Diagnosis of curvilinear relationships centers on examining a curvilinear pattern of the error terms. Curvilinearity is typically corrected by transforming the independent variable with which the dependent variable is curvilinearly related.

15. *What is heteroscedasticity? How does it affect the results of multiple regression? How can we detect and remedy heteroscedasticity?*

Heteroscedasticity is the problem of unequal variances of the error term. Unequal variances of the error term violate the assumption of the random distribution of the error term and cause the statistical significance of regression coefficients to be underestimated. Heteroscedasticity is graphically detected by examining the error term plot for unequal variances. Error terms are also plotted against each independent variable to determine which dependent-independent variable relationship is heteroscedastic. Often, a logarithmic transformation of both the dependent and independent variables sufficiently corrects the problem.

16. *Explain the concept of autocorrelation. How can it affect the results of multiple regression? Also, explain how autocorrelation is detected and how it is remedied.*

Adjacent, time-ordered values of observations are usually highly correlated with each other: knowledge of today's value is a good predictor of tomorrow's. Autocorrelation (also called serial correlation) increases the significance of regression coefficients. Autocorrelation can be detected by plotting the error term against time. It is formally detected by testing the Durbin-Watson test statistic: values close to 2 indicate the absence of serial correlation, whereas values closer to 0 and 4 may indicate serial correlation. Two approaches to correcting for serial correlation are (1) to add a trend variable to the model and (2) to test the model in first-order difference form.

17. *Why is accurate measurement important in multiple regression?*

Multiple regression assumes that variables are measured accurately; variables should be substantively valid and free from any systematic biases. Accurate measurement is especially important for the dependent variable because inaccurate measurement may render it impossible for independent variables to achieve requisite levels of statistical significance.

18. *Explain the importance of neither omitting relevant variables nor including irrelevant variables.*

The effect of *omitting a relevant variable* is to inflate the value of t-test test statistics of independent variables that are included. The omitted variable is a relevant control variable. The effect of *including irrelevant variables* is the opposite, to understate the importance of other independent variables. Theoretically irrelevant variables cannot be justified, no matter how statistically significant they may be.

CRITICAL THINKING

1. Evaluate and explain the following statement: "Multiple regression is no substitute for bivariate analysis."

_____

_____

_____

_____

_____

_____

2. **You are a program manager for a welfare agency. In workbook Chapter 14, Critical Thinking Exercise 5, you examined the relationship between the length of time that people receive welfare (in months) and their education (total years). Now you want to consider other variables that might also affect the length of unemployment. Table W15.1 lists categories of different factors that are hypothesized to be the most important in affecting the length of unemployment. Interpret and write up your results.**

_____
_____
_____
_____
_____
_____

Table W15.1 ———⌇⌇⌇— Multiple Regression Output

Model

R	R-square	Adjusted R^2	SEE
0.660	0.435	0.423	0.092

Dependent variable: Unemployment duration

ANOVA Table

Model	Sum of squares	df	Mean square	F	Sig.
Regression	6.294	5	1.259	146.867	0.000
Residual	2.726	318	0.008		
Total	9.020	323			

Coefficients

Model	Unstandardized coefficients		Standardized coefficients		
	b	SE	Beta	t	Sig.
Constant	0.231	.030		7.740	0.000
Receives job training	−0.010	.004	−0.088	−2.579	0.010
Marital status[a]	−0.072	.017	−0.830	−4.125	0.000
Medical condition	0.013	.005	0.140	2.540	0.012
Number of dependents	0.000	.001	0.008	0.252	0.802
Education	−0.003	.003	−0.030	−0.834	0.405

Note: SEE = standard error of the estimate; SE = standard error; Sig. = significance.
[a] Marital Status: 1 = married; 0 = not married.

3. **Develop a fully specified model of the factors that affect fundraising at a nonprofit, social services organization. Focus on different categories of factors that affect fundraising, and consider how some might be grouped as index variables.**

_____
_____
_____
_____
_____
_____

4. Develop a fully specified model of the factors that affect teenage violence in high schools.

5. Explain how regression can be used for prediction. What problem do you see with predicting dependent variable values based on independent variable values that lie outside the range of observations that have been used to estimate the model?

_____

_____

_____

_____

_____

_____

6. Consider a hypothetical variable Race, that is coded as 1 = Caucasian, 2 = Native American, 3 = African American, 4 = Asian or Pacific Islander, and 5 = Other. Recode this variable as a dummy variable that indicates whether the respondent is Caucasian.

_____

_____

_____

_____

_____

_____

7. Explain in your own words why the error term plot should show a random pattern. Also, which variables are shown on the axes?

_____

_____

_____

_____

_____

_____

8. Discuss, in practical terms, how analysts determine which observations are outliers. Discuss also how you would justify the deletion of observations that are outliers.

_____

_____

_____

_____

_____

_____

9. Draw an error term plot that shows the presence of an outlier (without peeking in the textbook!).

10. If two variables are highly correlated with each other (for example, $r^2 = 0.65$), does it follow that they are multicollinear, as well?

_____

_____

_____

_____

_____

_____

11. Explain the problem of including irrelevant variables.

_____

_____

_____

_____

_____

_____

12. Explain why time series data often lead to correlated error terms.

_____

_____

_____

_____

_____

_____

DATA-BASED EXERCISES

1. Consider the model shown in Table 15.1 of the textbook. In the Productivity dataset, the dependent variable is Productivity, and the independent variables are labeled, respectively, Teamwork, Jobknowl, Jobauthr, Wrkdyssk, and Recogawd. After you rerun the model shown in Table 15.1, create dummy variables for each of the four departments, and add to the model dummy variables for the first three departments. Are departments associated with employees' perceptions of productivity controlled for all other factors of the model? If yes, which departments are significantly associated with employees' perceptions of productivity? Record your answers on a separate sheet.

2. Use the Public Perceptions dataset. Examine a multiple regression model in which the dependent variable is Posview ("I have a positive view of Orange County"). The independent variables are Quality ("The quality of life in Orange County is good"), Interest ("I believe that the county is interested in what I have to say"), Respect ("The employees treated me with courtesy and respect"), Trust ("Do you trust Orange County to do what is right most of the time?"), and Works ("Do you believe that Orange County works efficiently?"). Examine the error term plot, and write up your findings. Record your answers on a separate sheet.

3. Regarding the model in Exercise 2, consider the effects of race and Hispanic origin on having a positive view. Do race and Hispanic origin affect overall perceptions, when controlled for other variables mentioned in the earlier exercise? Record your answers on a separate sheet.

4. Use the Time dataset. This exercise illustrates the problem of outliers. In this exercise, we examine the effect of water pollution on the concentration of fish in a lake. The dataset contains two variables, Fishcon (the concentration of fish) and Contam1 (the concentration of a water pollutant). The observations are drawn from different parts of a large lake in order to test the hypothesis that alleged water pollution is affecting the stock of fish.

   a. Examine and discuss whether the variables Fishcon and Contam1 are approximately normally distributed.

   _____

   _____

   _____

   _____

   _____

   b. Make a scatterplot of Fishcon and Contam1 for the purpose of getting a visual read of the relationship. Is the relationship positive or negative? Is it strong or weak? Are there any possible outliers? Print the output, and write up your answers.

   _____

   _____

   _____

   _____

   _____

   c. Based on your visual read, you wish to test the hypothesis that the two variables are related. Conduct a simple regression, with Fishcon as the dependent variable. Examine the error term plot for possible outliers. What do you conclude?

   _____

   _____

   _____

   _____

   _____

d. Identify the outlier, and eliminate it from subsequent analysis. Provide a write-up of the modified analysis that includes (1) the hypothesis, (2) the relationship between the variables ($y = ax + b$), (3) the identification and removal of outliers, (4) the correlation and percentage of variance explained (r and r^2), and (5) a plot of the standardized residuals against the predicted values of the dependent variable.

_____

_____

_____

_____

_____

5. **Use the Time dataset. This exercise illustrates the use of dummy variables and includes a test of multicollinearity. The dataset contains observations from 35 hypothetical cities regarding the use of citizen focus groups in various departments (Focus). The data are based on a survey. Most variables are index variables taken from different survey questions. The variables are defined as follows:**

Focus = A composite measure of the breadth and depth of the use of citizen focus groups in a city. Varies from 0 (low) to 20 (high).

Mgrint = A measure of the interest of the city manager in obtaining citizen-based feedback. Varies from 1 (low) to 4 (high).

Pubcompl = A measure of public complaints about the quality and effectiveness of a wide range of municipal services. Varies from 1 (low) to 8 (high).

Budget = Indicates whether municipal budgets have increased in the past two years. Values are −1 = decrease in budget; 0 = no change in budget; 1 = increase in budget.

Size = City size. Varies from 1 = small to 7 = large.

Region = An indicator variable of the region in which the city is located. Values: 1 = Northeast; 2 = South; 3 = Midwest; 4 = West.

In this analysis, you wish to understand which variables cause cities to use citizen-based focus groups.

a. Briefly state your hypotheses.

_____

_____

_____

_____

_____

b. Provide a brief description of variables (univariate analysis). Also, examine the bivariate associations between Focus and Mgrint, Pubcompl, Budget, and Size. Examine the bivariate relationships that exist between all possible pairs of these variables.

_____

_____

_____

_____

_____

c. Examine whether Mgrint, Pubcompl, Budget, and Size are statistically associated with the use of focus groups. For this purpose, conduct a multiple regression in which the dependent variable is Focus and the independent variables are Mgrint, Pubcompl, Budget, and Size. What do you conclude? (You need not write up these results.)

_____

_____

_____

_____

_____

d. You now wish to include the effect of region in your analysis. To do this, you must make Region a dummy variable. Assume you wish to compare the effect of the different regions with Midwest. To make the dummy variables for the Northeast, South, and West, you must either recode the data for each region or enter the data manually. Through either of these techniques, add Northeast, South, and West to your model and rerun the analysis.

_____

_____

_____

_____

_____

e. Provide a complete write-up of the regression. (1) Identify which variables are significant and at what level. Identify the adjusted R-square statistic (is it a strong or weak association?). Also, discuss the beta coefficients. What do you conclude? (2) Plot the standardized residuals against the standardized predicted values. What do you conclude? (3) To examine the possibility of multicollinearity, examine the bivariate correlations among the independent variables. What do you conclude? Given the significance of coefficients, is multicollinearity a problem here?

_____

_____

_____

_____

_____

6. **Use the Time dataset. This exercise illustrates the problem of nonlinearity. It is commonly hypothesized that crimes are more frequent in large cities. The dataset contains the following variables:**

Nvcrime = Index of nonviolent crimes in a given year.
Citysize = City size.

a. To test the above hypothesis, regress Nvcrime as a function of Citysize. Plot the standardized error term against the standardized predicted values and observe the curvilinear (parabolic) slope of the error terms.

_____

_____

_____

_____

_____

b. You suspect that this problem occurs because the relationship between the variables is nonlinear. To examine this possibility, plot Nvcrime against Citysize. Notice the faint rounded curve. Based on the nature of the curve, you decide that a transformation of Citysize is required. You decide to try a square root of Citysize. Make a square root transformation of Citysize. To evaluate the success of this transformation, plot the transformed variable, called TCity (on the X-axis), against Nvcrime (on the Y-axis). Is the relationship still nonlinear? Was the transformation successful?

_____

_____

_____

_____

_____

c. Next, rerun the regression using the transformed variable TCity. Hence, Nvcrime = f(TCity). Reevaluate the residuals by plotting the error term of the transformed model against the transformed independent variable, TCity. What pattern, if any, do you see? If the transformation was unsuccessful, try a log transformation. Do you see a pattern now?

_____

_____

_____

_____

_____

7. (*optional*) **Refer to Data-Based Exercise 7 in Chapter 14. Add a second independent variable and run a multiple regression that examines the impact of these two variables on your academic performance (the dependent variable). Perform related tests of regression assumptions. Interpret the results. What do you conclude? Write a report that summarizes your findings for a person who knows nothing about statistics.**

_____

_____

_____

_____

_____

FURTHER READING

Many statistics books discuss regression analysis, including those mentioned in previous chapters of this workbook. However, some of these discussions are a little superficial. For a brief introduction, see Larry Gonick and Woollcott Smith, *The Cartoon Guide to Statistics* (New York: HarperPerennial, 1994), or Sam Kash Kachigan, *Multivariate Statistical Analysis: A Conceptual Introduction*, 2nd ed. (New York: Radius Press, 1991).

For a more solid introduction, try William M. Mendenhall, *A Second Course in Statistics: Regression Analysis*, 6th ed. (Upper Saddle River, N.J.: Prentice Hall, 2003). Another good presentation is found in David G. Kleinbaum et al., *Applied Regression Analysis and Multivariable Methods* (Pacific Grove, Calif.: Duxbury Press, 1998). Try also J. McKee and J. McClendon, *Multiple Regression and Causal Analysis* (Long Grove, Ill.: Waveland Press, 2002).

The following books are a little advanced but also quite useful. Two classic textbooks with an economics orientation are Robert Pindyck and Daniel Rubinfield, *Econometric Models and Economic Forecasts*, 3rd ed. (New York: McGraw-Hill, 1997), and Damodar Gujarati, *Basic Econometrics*, 4th ed. (New York: McGraw-Hill, 2002). A well-respected general social science book is John Neter et al., *Applied Linear Statistical Models*, 4th ed. (New York: McGraw-Hill, 1996).

Logistic Regression

Q & A

1. When should logistic regression be used? Provide some examples.

Logistic regression should be used when the dependent variable is dichotomous, that is, when it has only two values. Some typical examples of a dichotomous dependent variable are whether or not someone got elected, whether or not a war occurred, and whether or not a medical event occurred. In these instances, something either happened, or it didn't—a dichotomous situation.

2. What regression problem does logistic regression address?

Multiple regression assumes a continuous dependent variable. Logistic regression uses a dichotomous dependent variable, that is, one that has only two values, such as zero and one.

3. How does the estimation model of logistic regression differ from multiple regression?

Whereas the multiple regression estimation model uses a straight line, logistic regression uses a logistic curve, which is S-shaped. Both approaches select a model that best fits the observed observations.

4. What is the log likelihood value, −2LL?

The log likelihood value, −2LL, is a quantitative measure of how well the model predicts observed values. Better-fitting models have smaller values of |−2LL|.

5. How is a classification table used to assess the goodness of fit in logistic regression?

A classification table shows the percentage of corrected predicted observations. The minimum is 50 percent, indicating the lack of any useful prediction. Typically, standards of 80–85 percent indicate good model prediction.

6. What are Nagelkerke R^2 and Cox and Snell R^2?

These are measures of association. Higher values imply a better fit. Nagelkerke R^2 has a variance-explained interpretation.

7. What test is used for the statistical significance of logistic regression coefficients?

In logistic regression, Wald chi-square is used as a test statistic to determine the statistical significance of logistic regression coefficients.

8. *How can logistic regression coefficients be used to calculate event probabilities?*

The predicted values of logistic regression coefficients can be used to show the probability of an event's occurring, by using the following formula:

$\text{Prob(event)} = 1/[1 + e^{-Z}]$, where $Z = a + b_1 x_1 + b_2 x_2 + \dots$

Z is also called the logit.

9. *What is an odds ratio?*

An odds ratio is used to compare the probability of something occurring, as compared to it not occurring. One way of using this measure is to observe how the odds ratio changes when only one independent variable is changed, such as by one unit.

CRITICAL THINKING

1. Identify dichotomous variables that are relevant to your area of interest, and develop a model to predict them.

_____

_____

_____

_____

_____

_____

2. Explain the following statement: "The dichotomous nature of the dependent variable violates an assumption of multiple regression."

_____

_____

_____

_____

_____

_____

3. The S-shaped logistic curve has values that lie between 0 and 1. What problem does this address?

_____

_____

_____

_____

_____

_____

4. Explain why a good model fit will show a Hosmer and Lemeshow test statistic that is insignificant.

_____

_____

_____

_____

_____

_____

5. Verify the event probability calculations shown in Table 16.2 of the textbook.

_____

_____

_____

_____

_____

_____

6. Table W16.1 shows the output of a logistic model that predicts promotion within five years. Is the model adequate: why, or why not? What is the probability that a 37-year-old female who has a performance appraisal rating of 4 will be promoted? The performance variable (Appraisal) is measured on a scale of 5 = high to 1 = low; Gender is defined as 1 = male, 2 = female; and Age = employee's age (in years).

Table W16.1 ————— Logistic Regression Output

Model Fit

2 log likelihood (−2LL)		Cox and Snell R^2	Nagelkerke R^2	Hosmer and Lemeshow test	
Model	Sig. (base model)			Chi-square	Sig.
48.253	0.000	0.317	0.428	4.940	0.764

Dependent variable: Promotion

Coefficients

Model	Unstandardized coefficients		Wald chi-square	Sign.
	b	SE		
Constant	−4.016	3.285	1.495	0.221
Gender	−0.532	0.734	0.526	0.468
Appraisal	1.990	0.603	10.878	0.001
Age	−0.082	0.083	0.977	0.323

Classification Table

Observed		Predicted		
		Promotion		Percentage
Variable	Group	0	1	correct
Promotion	0	23	7	76.7
	1	6	14	70.0
Overall percentage				74.0

Note: Sig. = significance; SE = standard error

7. Identify one or more research articles that use logistic regression. Record your findings on a separate sheet.

DATA-BASED EXERCISES

1. Use the Public Perceptions dataset. Predict Trust ("Trust in government") as a function of Interest ("County officials are interested in what I have to say"), Works ("Do you believe the county government works efficiently?"), Quality ("The quality of life in Orange County is good"), and race. To this

end, (1) create a dummy variable for race (1 = white, 0 = all others) from the variable Ethnic, and (2) recode the values of "DK" for the variables Trust and Works as missing. Use logistic regression, and report the results.

Trust = f(Interest, Works, Quality, White)

a. Verify that the dependent variable is dichotomous.

_____

_____

_____

b. Does the model satisfy the standard for correctly predicted observations?

_____

_____

_____

c. Which variables are significant?

_____

_____

_____

d. Calculate event probabilities.

_____

_____

_____

2. **Use the Public Perceptions dataset. Predict Manage ("Doing a good job managing growth") as a function of Works ("Do you believe the county government works efficiently?"), Quality ("The quality of life in Orange County is good"), and Watch ("Watching Orange County TV"). Use logistic regression, and report the results.**

Manage = f(Works, Quality, Watch).

a. Verify that the dependent variable is dichotomous.

_____

_____

_____

b. Does the model satisfy the standard for correctly predicted observations? If not, does it satisfy the Hosmer and Lemeshow test?

_____

_____

_____

c. Which variables are significant?

_____

_____

_____

d. Calculate event probabilities.

_____

_____

_____

3. Political scientists often use logistic regression for modeling factors affecting election outcomes. Some of these datasets are available online. Search for these on Google, by using the search string "political elections SPSS data," for example, if you are using SPSS.

    One of the sites that host election datasets is at the University of Essex (England), Project on Political Transformation and the Electoral Process in Post-Communist Europe (www.essex.ac.uk/elections). For example, consider the SPSS dataset regarding Russian candidates in 1999 elections. At this website, select Candidate data (from the left scroll bar) → Russia → 1999 SPSS format. (If you do not use SPSS, you should save this file to your computer, and then use your own statistical software program to open the file.) Open the saved file, and predict, for example, factors associated with candidates winning elections. You may need to first transform this variable to 0 = not winning an election and 1 = winning an election, as this dataset distinguishes between being elected in a single-member constituency (coded 1) and being elected from a party list (coded 2). How is being an incumbent associated with winning elections in Russia?

    _____

    _____

    _____

    _____

    _____

4. Visit the University of Michigan Library, "Statistical Resources on the Web Political Science" site (www.lib.umich.edu/govdocs/stpolisc.html#nes). Examine some of the available datasets (for example, on elections). Another resource is the University of California, which makes datasets available through SDA, Survey Documentation & Analysis (http://sda.berkeley.edu). Explore available datasets through the link "SDA archive." Select any dataset (for example, National Election Survey 1948–2000), and note the option to run logit regression. However, you should first examine the variable descriptions by selecting "Open Extra Codebook Window." You will likely need to recode some of the variables first. You can also download a customized subset of data.

FURTHER READING

Numerous advanced texts are available on the topics discussed in this chapter. For a discussion of logistic regression, see Joseph Hair et al., *Multivariate Data Analysis* (Upper Saddle River, N.J.: Prentice Hall, 1998). This is an advanced, but nonmathematical introduction. Another text is David Hosmer and Stanley Lemeshow, *Applied Logistic Regression* (New York: Wiley, 2000). Many of the previously mentioned texts that discuss regression also cover logistic regression.

The research literature includes many examples of logistic regression. Here are some: John Ishiyama, "Does Globalization Breed Ethnic Conflict?" *Nationalism & Ethnic Politics* 9 (winter 2003): 1–23; Matthew J. Dickinson and Kathryn Dunn Tenpas, "Explaining Increasing Turnover Rates Among Presidential Advisers, 1929–1997," *Journal of Politics* (May 1997): 434–449; P. Edward French, Sangho Moon, and Rodney E. Stanley, "Utilizing Logistic Regression for Explaining Lottery Adoption in the Volunteer State," *International Journal of Public Administration* 27 (2004): 353–367; and Marc A. Wallace, "An Analysis of Presidential Preferences in the Distribution of Empowerment Zones and Enterprise Communities," *Public Administration Review* 63 (2003): 562–572. You can readily use databases available through your library to find others.

Time Series Analysis

Q & A

1. What are time series data?

Time series data are data that have been collected over time, such as periodic assessments of performance outcomes or public (or client) opinions.

2. Which regression assumption is usually violated when using time series data? What problem does this cause?

With time series data, the assumption of random distribution of error terms usually is violated. Specifically, the error term plot, when plotted against the sequence of time-ordered observations, typically exhibits a pattern. This is called autocorrelation or serial correlation. The problem with autocorrelation is that it severely exaggerates the statistical significance of variables, leading to the erroneous conclusion that variables are statistically associated when they are not.

3. How is autocorrelation detected?

Autocorrelation can be detected by plotting the error term against time. It is formally detected by testing the Durbin-Watson test statistic: values close to 2 indicate the absence of serial correlation, whereas values closer to 0 and 4 may indicate serial correlation.

4. How is autocorrelation addressed?

Two strategies are available for correcting serial correlation: the first strategy is to add a trend variable to the model, and the second strategy is to examine the relationship in so-called first-order differences. Relationships in first-difference form often eliminate problems of serial correlation because differenced data exhibit far more variability than do levels data. By contrast, adding a trend variable is a prophylactic strategy that attempts to control for the problem. Regression of first-order differences is considered a more stringent test.

5. How is time series regression used for evaluating the impact of policies?

Time series data are excellent for evaluating the impact of a policy or program. Levels of performance or service utilization are tracked and compared with the moment or period in which a policy is implemented.

6. What are policy variables?

Policy variables measure when and how policies affect the dependent variables. Four types of policy variables are those that model pulse, period, step, and increasing impacts.

7. *What are lagged variables?*

Lagged variables are independent variables that have a lagged effect on the dependent variable.

8. *Explain the difference between predicted values and forecasted values.*

Predicted values are calculated values (based on the regression coefficients) of the dependent variable that can be compared with the actual (observed) values of the dependent variable. Forecasted values are calculated values of a variable for a future time for which no observed value has yet occurred. Hence, forecasted values cannot be compared with observed values.

9. *What strategy is used to validate forecasts?*

Forecasts of the current period(s) are made using observations from preceding periods. These forecasts are then compared with actual observations.

10. *Name four types of regression-based forecasting.*

Regression-based forecasting includes leading indicators, curve estimation, exponential smoothing, and ARIMA.

11. *What is forecasting with leading indicators?*

Forecasting with leading indicators involves regression with independent variables that are all lagged (leading indicators). These leading indicators are then regarded as harbingers of future change.

12. *What is the difference between curve estimation and exponential smoothing?*

Curve estimation makes forecasts based only on the level and trend variable. Exponential smoothing uses an iterative estimation process that chooses parameters of level, trend, and seasonality to best fit a model to the observed data.

13. *How are periodic effects included in forecasts?*

Periodicity is included in forecasts by adjusting mean forecasts to reflect the mean periodicity effects of prior periods.

14. *Compare forecasting based on prior moving averages, prior moving changes, and known ratios.*

Forecasting based on prior moving averages predicts future values based on the mean of preceding values. Forecasting based on prior moving changes predicts future values based on the immediately preceding value and the mean of preceding increases. Forecasting based on known ratios uses the value of one variable to predict another variable, assuming that both the ratio of variables and an accurate forecast of the other variable are known. Forecasts based on prior moving averages tend to be conservative.

CRITICAL THINKING

1. **Give some examples of time series data in your area of interest. Discuss ways in which these data might be analyzed.**

_____

_____

_____

_____

_____

_____

2. Explain why autocorrelation is almost always present when using regression analysis with time series data.

_____

_____

_____

_____

_____

_____

3. The Durbin-Watson test statistic for autocorrelation of a regression model with 35 observations and four independent variables is 1.98. What do you conclude? And what would you conclude if the Durbin-Watson test statistic were 1.08?

_____

_____

_____

_____

_____

_____

4. Explain the following statement: "The regression of first-order differences is considered a far more stringent test than adding a trend variable."

_____

_____

_____

_____

_____

_____

5. Explain how policy variables help to evaluate program effectiveness. Does the magnitude of these dummy variables matter?

_____

_____

_____

_____

_____

_____

6. Give an example of an independent variable that you suspect might have a lagged impact on a dependent variable.

_____

_____

_____

_____

_____

_____

7. **Explain the difference between prediction and forecasting.**

_____
_____
_____
_____
_____
_____
_____

8. **Discuss why prior moving averages (PMA) forecasting may be more conservative than forecasting based on prior average changes.**

_____
_____
_____
_____
_____
_____
_____

9. **Discuss the steps for forecasting with periodic effects with few observations.**

_____
_____
_____
_____
_____
_____
_____

10. **Consider the trend shown in Figure W17.1. Should forecasting involve periodicity, and, if so, what period of time should be considered? What is the consequence of not using periodicity?**

_____
_____
_____
_____
_____
_____

Figure W17.1 ———— ᐞᴧᐞ Trend

11. **How might you forecast the revenues of a city? Identify three different approaches.**

_____
_____
_____
_____
_____

DATA-BASED EXERCISES

1. **Use the Time dataset. This exercise illustrates the autocorrelation problem in the use of policy variables. Time series data are common in program evaluation and public policy. These data examine the impact of a law, which, among other things, increases jail time for those convicted of driving under the influence (DUI). The dataset contains the following variables:**

   Fatal = Traffic fatalities per 100,000 miles driven.

   Year = Year of traffic fatalities measured.

   Short = A dummy variable identifying when the policy intervention occurred, namely, in 1980 when a law was passed that requires mandatory jail time for DUI.

   The values are 0 = pre–law adoption (pre-1980) and 1 = post–law adoption (post-1980).

   Long = A dummy variable identifying the number of years of post–policy adoption. The values are 0 for pre–law adoption, and 1 for 1980, 2 for 1981, 3 for 1982, and so forth. This variable gives weight to the long-term effect of policy.

   Jailtime = Days of jail time served by offenders as a result of the law.

   Note: Although increased jail time is the primary effect of the program, data from other aspects of the program (such as midnight checkpoints) are not available to the researcher. The variables Short and Long model these unknown effects.

   a. You wish to evaluate whether the new law has been effective. You model the effect on fatalities and explore the possibility of autocorrelation in time series data. Hence, Fatal = f(Short, Long, Jailtime). Run the regression analysis, and examine the error term for autocorrelation. Specifically, examine the Durbin-Watson test statistic. What do you conclude?

   _____

   _____

   _____

   _____

   _____

   b. Now, take the trend variable into account: Add Year as an independent variable to your list. Again, note the Durbin-Watson statistic. What do you conclude about adding the trend variable? Provide a complete write-up.

   _____

   _____

   _____

   _____

   _____

   c. For further rigor, you examine the relationship in first-order differences. Make first-order differences, and examine ΔFatal = f(Short, Long, ΔJailtime). What do you conclude? Also, try lagging each of the independent variables for up to two periods. What do you conclude?

   _____

   _____

   _____

   _____

   _____

2. **Use the Crime dataset. The data are monthly observations of juvenile arrests in a city with a curfew for teenagers. The curfew prohibits teenagers from being outside between 8 p.m. and 1 a.m.**

Note: These data are adapted from actual cities. Although these are monthly data, the same approach can be applied to weekly or daily data. In those cases, rather than controlling periodicity by month, control variables control for periodicity by week or day.

a. Plot the number of juvenile arrests (Juvarsts) over time. What do you conclude about the impact of the curfew? What factors might underlie the periodicity?

_____

_____

_____

_____

_____

b. Run the regression of Curfew against Juvarsts. What do you conclude from the Durbin-Watson statistic? To attempt to correct for autocorrelation, include both the year and each of the months as control variables. Run the model in both levels and first-order difference forms, hence:

$$\text{Juvarsts} = f(\text{Curfew, Month 1} - \text{Month 11, Year}), \text{ and}$$

$$\Delta\text{Juvarsts} = f(\Delta\text{Curfew, Month 1} - \text{Month 11, Year}).$$

Which of these models deals with the problem of autocorrelation? Why is Month 12 excluded from the model?

_____

_____

_____

_____

_____

c. It is sometimes noted in the literature that law enforcement displaces crime rather than reduces it. Rather than committing crimes between 8 p.m. and 1 a.m., juveniles will target other time periods to commit crimes. The dataset includes the variable Crimarst, which measures total monthly juvenile arrests. Run the same models as under item b, with Crimarst as the dependent variable. What do you conclude?

_____

_____

_____

_____

_____

3. **Table W17.1 shows expenditures for the past five years. Forecast the next three periods using (1) prior moving averages (three-year spans), and (2) prior average moving changes (with last period as base). Add your forecast to the table.**

Table W17.1 ⸺⌇⌇⌇⸺ Worksheet for Forecasting Based on Prior Moving Changes

Time	Expenditures (current $s)	Inflation (%)	Expenditures (constant $s)	Increase	Avg. changes	Forecasts
1	100	4.1	?	—	—	—
2	102	3.0	?	?	—	—
3	108	2.4	114.1	?	—	—
4	112	3.2	115.6	?	?	—
5	116	—	116.0	?	?	?
6	—	—	—	?	?	?
7	—	—	—	?	?	?
8	—	—	—	—	—	?

4. Table W17.2 shows attendance data of a public museum. Make a worksheet for calculating forecasts based on (1) prior moving averages and (2) prior moving changes for the next five periods. Also, validate your forecasts by comparing actual and predicted values.

_____

_____

_____

_____

_____

Table W17.2 ———————— Public Museum Attendance

Time	Attendance	Time	Attendance
1	1,205	9	1,468
2	1,309	10	1,602
3	1,325	11	1,625
4	1,226	12	1,698
5	1,450	13	1,550
6	1,529	14	1,623
7	1,679	15	1,708
8	1,543	16	1,767

5. Use linear regression to forecast museum attendance based on the data provided in the preceding exercise.

_____

_____

_____

_____

_____

6. Daily workload activities are shown in Table W17.3. Forecast workloads for Week 5.

Table W17.3 ———————— Daily Workload Activity

Day	Workload	Day	Workload	Day	Workload
1	63	6	70	11	69
2	72	7	77	12	75
3	76	8	75	13	77
4	67	9	72	14	70
5	53	10	50	15	62

7. Use the Crime dataset. (1) Create a new variable, Juvars2, which is the number of juvenile arrests between 8 p.m. and 1 a.m. (Juvarsts) prior to the curfew. (2) Use curve estimation to forecast future arrest rates. Using alternative models, what do you conclude about likely future arrest rates? (3) To include periodicity effects, try to forecast using exponential smoothing. (*Note:* This procedure is not available on all statistical software.) Record your findings on a separate sheet.

8. A regulatory analyst examines violations. The data in Table W17.4 show the occurrence of the first violation as a function of the number of years of being in business. Create a spreadsheet that reflects these data and determine the probability of violation in each period.

Table W17.4 ——————〜〜〜— First Violations as a Function of Years in the Business

Year	No. of businesses	No. of violations
0	10	0
1	12	8
2	15	2
3	18	3
4	24	2
5	12	4
6	15	1

FURTHER READING

Discussions of time series regression tend to be heavily mathematical, but many textbooks do provide a good conceptual foundation. See William M. Mendenhall, *A Second Course in Statistics: Regression Analysis,* 6th ed. (Upper Saddle River, N.J.: Prentice Hall, 2003). Some useful chapters are in Gerald Miller and Marcia Whicker, *Handbook of Research Methods in Public Administration* (New York: Marcel Dekker, 1999), chaps. 14 through 16. You can also look for articles using time series regression in your field of interest.

For forecasting, see S. Makradakis, *Forecasting* (New York: Wiley, 1998). Also, SPSS, *Trends 10.0* (Chicago: SPSS, Inc., 1999) provides numerous illustrations and examples. The Trends module is marketed separately from other software. Forecasting, as discussed here, is also found in Murray Spiegel and Larry Stephens, *Statistics: Schaum's Outline Series* (New York: McGraw-Hill, 1998). You can also look at examples of forecasting, such as U.S. Congressional Budget Office, *The Budget and Economic Outlook: Fiscal Years 2006 to 2015* (Washington, D.C.: U.S. Congressional Budget Office, 2005).

18

Survey of Other Techniques

Q & A

1. What is path analysis, and what advantage does it offer over multiple regression?

Path analysis is a causal modeling technique. Unlike multiple regression, path analysis allows for direct and indirect effects of variables. Path analysis is a recursive causal modeling technique, that is, one that does not allow feedback loops.

2. How are paths estimated?

Each path is estimated separately using regression (ordinary least squares, or OLS).

3. What is an exogenous variable? What is an endogenous variable? What purpose do these terms serve?

Causal modeling distinguishes between *exogenous* variables, which are variables that are unaffected by other variables in the model, and *endogenous* variables, which are affected by other variables. The distinction is useful because in causal models variables can be both independent and dependent.

4. What assumptions must path analysis models satisfy?

Path analysis must satisfy all OLS assumptions (see Chapter 1 in the textbook). In addition, all error terms must be uncorrelated with all exogenous variables. As in regression, the model must be theory based.

5. How are direct and indirect effects of variables calculated?

Direct effects are simply the beta coefficients of the variables that immediately affect another variable. Indirect effects are calculated as the product of beta coefficients of each pathway. See Table 18.1 in the textbook for an example of such calculations.

6. What is a structural equation model, and how is it different from path analysis?

Structural equation models simultaneously estimate relationships among observed variables and factor constructs. Unlike path analysis, structural equation models may involve feedback loops. Models with feedback loops are called nonrecursive.

7. What are censored data? Give an example.

Censored observations are those for which the specified outcomes have yet to occur. For example, in a study of student retention, some students have not (yet) dropped out of the program but may still do so before they graduate.

8. *What is the purpose of a life table?*

Life tables show the probability of a dichotomous event's occurring for each time period.

9. *What is factor analysis?*

Factor analysis is an exploratory technique that groups variables together based on their similarities and dissimilarities. Similarly grouped variables may suggest variables for subsequent index construction.

10. *What four steps does factor analysis involve?*

(1) Determining that the group of variables has enough correlation to allow for factor analysis
(2) Determining how many factors should be used for classifying (or grouping) the variables
(3) Improving the interpretation of correlations and factors (through a process called rotation)
(4) Naming the factors and, possibly, creating index variables for subsequent analysis

CRITICAL THINKING

1. **Draw a recursive causal model (path analysis) of factors that increase student success, measured as graduation. Which variables are direct influences, which are indirect influences, and which, if any, are both? Be sure to indicate clearly the direct and indirect influences on the dependent variable.**

2. **Figure W18.1 shows the results of a path analysis. The values above the paths are beta coefficients. Which variable has the largest influence?**

Figure W18.1 —∿— Path Analysis with Beta Coefficients

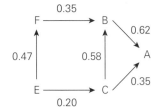

3. **Give three examples of situations that may involve censored data.**

4. Do censored data necessarily involve data that are collected over time?

_____

_____

_____

_____

_____

_____

5. Give an example of a leading indicator of crime that might be used in regression-based forecasting.

_____

_____

_____

_____

_____

_____

DATA-BASED EXERCISE

1. Use the Productivity dataset. Create a path analysis of the model shown in Figure W18.2. Does the model meet the condition of not having feedback loops? Begin by specifying (that is, identifying) all the regression models that are to be estimated. For each, identify the dependent and independent variables. Then estimate ("run") the models, record the beta coefficients, and calculate direct and indirect effects.

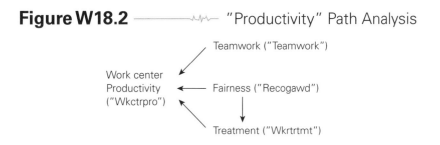

Figure W18.2 ⸺⌇⸺ "Productivity" Path Analysis

FURTHER READING

For a discussion of various exploratory techniques, see Sam Kash Kachigan, *Multivariate Statistical Analysis: A Conceptual Introduction,* 2nd ed. (New York: Radius Press, 1991). See also Joseph Hair et al., *Multivariate Data Analysis,* 7th ed. (Upper Saddle River, N.J.: Prentice Hall, 2009) for a more advanced discussion. This book also has an excellent, introductory chapter on ANOVA.

For survival analysis, see David Hosmer and Stanley Lemeshow, *Applied Survival Analysis: Regression Modeling of Time to Event Data* (New York: Wiley, 2008); or *SPSS Advanced Models 16.0* (Chicago: SPSS, Inc.), available online. For structural equation models, the *AMOS 17.0 User's Guide* (Chicago: SPSS, Inc., 2005) provides a useful introduction and many clear examples, available online. AMOS is very user friendly.

A free student download of this software with sample datasets is available at www.amosdevelopment.com. For an example of research using this technique, see J. West and E. Berman, "The Impact of Bad Management Work Habits on Public Sector Performance: A Study of Local Government Managers," *Public Personnel Management* 40 (2011): 63–87.

CHAPTER

19

Excel User's Guide

This chapter provides a guide on how to use Microsoft Excel in calculations and graphic presentations. We assume that you have basic knowledge about Excel, which is popular and easy-to-use spreadsheet software. If you are not comfortable with the software, visit the Microsoft Office website to take a tutorial or read an introductory guide to using Excel.

All Excel calculations introduced in this chapter are conducted with either Data Analysis ToolPak or the Insert Function (f_x) button. Although Excel examples in this chapter were prepared using Excel 2010 or 2007, the instructions in this book apply to Excel 2003, too.

LOADING THE DATA ANALYSIS TOOLPAK

To use the Data Analysis ToolPak, you need to load it first. To load it in Excel 2010, click the File tab, and then click Options. Click Add-Ins, and then in the Manage box, select Excel Add-Ins. Click Go. In the Add-Ins available box, select the Analysis ToolPak check box, and then click OK. If Analysis ToolPak is not listed in the Add-Ins available box, click Browse to locate it. If you see a message that the Analysis ToolPak is not currently installed on your computer, click Yes to install it when prompted to do so. After you load the Analysis ToolPak, the Data Analysis command is available in the Analysis group on the Data tab.

To load the Analysis ToolPak in Excel 2007, click the Microsoft Office Button, often located at the upper left-hand corner of your Excel sheet, and then click Excel Options. Click Add-Ins, and then in the Manage Box, select Excel Add-Ins. In the Add-Ins available box, select the Analysis ToolPak check box, and click OK. If the Analysis ToolPak is not listed in the Add-Ins available box, click Browse to locate it. After you load the Analysis ToolPak, the Data Analysis command is available in the Analysis group on the Data tab.

To load the Analysis Toolpak in Excel 2003, on the Tools menu, click Add-Ins. In the Add-Ins available box, select the check box next to Analysis Toolpak, and then click OK. If the Toolpak is not listed, click Browse to locate it. You may see a message that says that Analysis Toolpak is not currently installed on your computer and asks you to install it. After you load the Analysis Toolpak, the Data Analysis command is available on the Tool menu.

LOCATING THE INSERT FUNCTION (F_x)

You should be able to easily locate the Insert Function button, labeled with symbol f_x, next to the Formula Bar in an Excel sheet. If your Excel sheet does not show it, click the View tab, and check the Formula Bar button in the Show/Hide group. You should also find it in the Function Library group on the Formulas tab. For Excel 2003 users who can't find it in an Excel sheet, click the Function button on the Insert tab.

THE EXCEL SHEET SCREEN AND DESCRIPTIVE STATISTICS PROCEDURE

To use Excel, you need to open an Excel sheet. Notice that a sheet is designed for data input in columns and rows. Columns are named by letter; rows are named by number. A particular cell can be located by using a letter and a number such as A1, B2, etc. Screen W19.1 shows the number of training courses completed by 20 participants in a job training program. The data are presented in a new Excel sheet. Notice that the first row of the sheet can be used for the labels of the variables, "Participant ID" in A1 and "Number of Courses Completed" in B1 in this example.

Excel makes it very easy to calculate and present the measures of central tendency and dispersion. You can use the Descriptive procedure in the Data Analysis ToolPak to obtain a group of such measures. Let's use the job training data as an example to illustrate this procedure. In a new Excel sheet, input the data on the number of courses completed in Column B as shown in Screen W19.2. Click the Data Analysis command in the Analysis Group on the Data tab if you use Excel 2010 or Excel 2007. If you use Excel 2003, click Data Analysis in the Tool menu. Select Descriptive Statistics in the Data Analysis window. Select the data in B1 to B21 in the Input Range (i.e., $B$1:$B$21). Click the Label in First Row box to show the number of courses completed as the title of your output. Select an Output Range that does not overlap with the data ($D$20 in this example). If you want your results in a new worksheet, select New Worksheet Ply instead of Output Range. Select Summary Statistics. Click OK. The results, shown in Screen W19.2., include the mean, median, mode, standard deviation, standard error, sample variance, range, sum, kurtosis, and skewness.

The Data Analysis Descriptive Statistics procedure gives a group of descriptive measures. If you want to obtain just one measure, for example, the mean, Excel Insert Function (f_x) provides a much easier and more convenient way to do so. Let's say that you want to calculate the mean for the number of courses completed in the preceding example. Click the Insert Function (f_x) button, next to the formula bar, to open the Insert Function dialog box, shown in Screen W19.3. In the Insert Function dialog box, if you know the name of the

Screen W19.1 ⎯⎯⎯⎯⎯⎯ A Screen of Excel Sheet

Screen W19.2 —— ∿∿ —— The Excel Descriptive Statistics Procedure

Screen W19.3 —— ∿∿ —— Insert Function Dialog Box

Screen W19.4 ———〜〜— Insert Function Argument Box

Function Arguments	? ×

AVERAGE

Number1	B2:B21|	▦	= {3;3;4;4;1;2;2;3;3;1;3;5;2;4;3;4;1;...
Number2		▦	= number

= 2.85

Returns the average (arithmetic mean) of its arguments, which can be numbers or names, arrays, or references that contain numbers.

Number1: number1,number2,... are 1 to 255 numeric arguments for which you want the average.

Formula result = 2.85

Help on this function   OK   Cancel

---

function you want to use, type the name in the Search for a Function window. If you don't know the name, select a category of formulas you want to work with from the Select a Category window. If you are not sure which category you should use, select the All category. Then click a function from the Select a Function window and read the definition of the function given below the window. Because you want to calculate the average of the data, scroll to the AVERAGE function. Select it and then click OK.

In the Function Arguments box, select data in cells from B2 to B21 (i.e., B2:B21) in the Number 1 window (the only calculation in this example). You should be able to see the 2.85 in the Formula Result, shown as in Screen W19.4. Click OK. The result should appear in a cell of your choice. You should also see the =AVERAGE (B2:B21) in the Formula Bar. In other words, you can use the Formula Bar directly to get your answer if you know the name of the function and the location of the data. Make sure you type the symbol "=" each time you use the Formula Bar and place a bracket "( )" for the data.

The Excel Insert Function is a very useful calculation tool. You can use it for many calculations in this book. Table W19.1 lists the names of some popular Insert Functions.

Excel offers another easy way to access statistical functions. Click Formulas and More Functions, as shown in Screen W19.5, to choose the statistical procedure you want. If you right-click on Statistical, you add a quick access button to Quick Access Toolbar.

Table W19.1 ———〜〜— Some Useful Excel Insert Functions (f_x)

Function	Name of Function in Excel
Mean	AVERAGE
Median	MEDIAN
Mode	MODE
Variance for a sample	VAR
Standard deviation for a sample	STDEV
Maximum	MAX
Minimum	MIN

Screen W19.5 ――――〜〜〜― Quick Access to Statistical Functions in Excel

FREQUENCY DISTRIBUTIONS

The Excel Data Analysis Histogram procedure allows easy calculation of frequencies and cumulative percentages. Let's use the job training course completion data in the preceding example to illustrate the procedure. In the data sheet, as shown in Screen W19.6, click the Data Analysis command in the Analysis Group on the Data tab. Select Histogram in the Data Analysis window. Select the number of courses completed in the Input Range (i.e., $B$1:$B$21). Determine the intervals in which you want to calculate the frequencies. In our example, we want the frequencies of all possible numbers in the number of courses completed (i.e., 1, 2, 3, 4, and 5). We create a new variable (Interval) to hold these numbers and Bin in the Histogram Procedure is the place to define the intervals. Select an Output Range that does not overlap with the data. If you want your results in a new worksheet, select New Worksheet Ply instead of Output Range. Click the Label box. This allows you to show the title of your output. (*Important:* If you do not select the title cells, B1 and C1 in this case, in the Input Range and Bin Range, then you do not want to check the Label box). Select Cumulative Percentage. Click OK. You should see the output as shown in Screen W19.6. Excel calculates the frequencies and cumulative percentages. Notice that it also creates in the "Interval" column of the frequency and cumulative percentage chart a "More" category for more than 5 courses completed.

If you want, you can also calculate a set of ranges for the number of courses completed, such as 0 to 3, 4 to 5, and above 5. Keep in mind that you need to enter the upper bound, not the lower bound, of an interval because Excel interprets the upper bound of a range as the lower bound of the next range. Screen W19.7 shows frequencies and cumulative percentages of such an example. The result shows that 70 percent (14 of 20) of participants completed three or fewer courses in the program.

Screen W19.6 ――――~∿∿~―― Calculating Frequencies and Cumulative Percentages

Screen W19.7 ――――~∿∿~―― Calculating Frequencies and Cumulative Percentages of Ranges

Screen W19.8 ──〜〜── Using CHITEST to Perform Chi-Square Test

CHI-SQUARE TEST

The CHITEST procedure in Excel Insert Function (f_x) allows easy calculation of the probability associated with a critical value, facilitating the chi-square hypothesis testing process. To illustrate this procedure, let's use the data on promotion by gender shown in Table 10.3 of the textbook. To use CHITEST, you need to obtain observed frequencies and expected frequencies as presented in Screen W19.8. In the CHITEST function arguments window, select observed frequencies in Actual_range (B4:C7 in our example) and expected frequencies in Expected_range (F4:G7 in our example). The formula result of 0.0296 is the probability associated with the critical value of the chi-square test. Because this value is smaller than 0.05, the result is statistically significant at the 5 percent level. Although the CHITEST procedure does not present the critical value, the associated probability provides the same information on the test result. It indicates that the relationship between promotion and gender exists.

ONE-SAMPLE T-TEST

Excel has procedures that allow you to perform one-sample and two-sample t-tests. The TDIST procedure in Insert Function can be used to calculate the probability associated with a critical t-value and can be used in a one-sample t-test. Screen W19.9 shows the procedure to obtain the probability using an example given in the discussion of one-sample testing in Chapter 12 in which the t-value is 2.43 with degrees of freedom of 9. In the TDIST procedure, the t-value needs to be placed in the X window (2.43, in this example). The result shows that the probability is 0.0380 with a two-tailed test. Excel does not take negative t-values, for some

Screen W19.9 ———— ⌇⌇⌇ ———— One-Sample T-Test

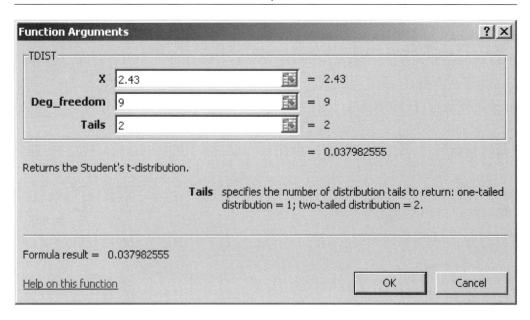

reason. However, because the t-distribution is symmetric, the probability value is the same for either a positive or a negative value. Thus you can use a positive value (say, 3.330) to replace the negative value of the same number (−3.330).

TWO-SAMPLES T-TEST

Excel Insert Function TTEST procedure is designed to perform t-tests of two sample means. Table W19.2 shows the psychosocial performances of 10 school-age participants in a nonprofit program designed to improve at-risk participants' psychosocial behaviors. The training performance is measured by a standardized test score on psychosocial behaviors; 100 is the best possible score and 50 is the worst.

Because the tests were performed on the same subjects, the results constitute a paired sample. Screen W19.10 shows the TTEST procedure with this sample. In the TTEST function arguments window, include before-training scores in Array 1 and after-training scores in Array 2. Choose a two-tailed test if you don't know the direction of the test. Type "1" in the window that says "Type" for the paired-samples test.

Table W19.2 ———— ⌇⌇⌇ ———— Training Performance for a Behavior Improvement Program

Training Participant ID	Before Training	After Training	Difference
1	85	89	4
2	67	73	6
3	83	81	−2
4	67	75	8
5	75	83	8
6	62	79	17
7	71	70	−1
8	71	79	8
9	82	82	0
10	59	70	11

Screen W19.10 ——∿∿— TTEST for a Paired-Samples T-Test

The result, probability or p = .0113, indicates that the difference between the average scores before and after the training is statistically significant at the 5 percent level.

The Excel Data Analysis t-Test procedure can also be used in hypothesis testing of two samples. Choose Data Analysis from the Data tab. Choose t-Test: Paired Two Sample for Means in the Data Analysis window. As shown in Screen W19.11, use the Variable 1 Range and Variable 2 Range windows for before and after training scores, respectively. The Hypothesized Mean Difference is 0 (meaning that there is no difference between the mean scores before and after the training). Check the Labels box if you include the variable names in the data input ranges. We set the alpha, the significance level, at .05. The output of the Data Analysis t-Test procedure provides much richer information than the Insert Function TTEST procedure. In addition to the means and variances of the samples, the results include the t-value of the two samples, the critical t-values for one-tailed and two-tailed tests, and their associated p-values.

T-tests for two independent sample means can be performed similarly. In the Insert Function TTEST procedure, as shown in Screen W19.12, choose 2 in the "Type" window from the function arguments window if equal variances is assumed for the two samples (homogeneity of variance) or choose 3 if unequal variances is assumed (heterogeneity of variance). The Data Analysis t-Test procedure allows you to choose t-Test with Two-Sample Assuming Equal Variance or t-Test with Two-Sample Assuming Unequal Variance. The Excel procedure for these two tests is the same as that for the paired-samples test.

Screen W19.11 ——— ⌇⌇⌇ Data Analysis t-Test for Paired Samples

Screen W19.12 ——— ⌇⌇⌇ TTEST Function Arguments Window

ANOVA

If you have more than two sample means and want to perform a one-way ANOVA, you can use the Excel Data Analysis ANOVA: Single Factor procedure. Consider an example. A city administration organizes a water-conservation campaign to educate residents on the need to conserve water. The campaign is conducted in three residential areas of the city. To determine the effectiveness of different educational instruments, the city provides flyers to the residents in area 1, flyers and a television ad in area 2, and only a television ad in area 3. Residents in the three areas are then tested to gauge their awareness of the need for water conservation. On the 10-point test used, a score of 10 corresponds to the highest level of awareness and a score of 0, to the lowest level. A sample from each area is drawn and the data are shown in Table W19.3.

In the Excel Data Analysis Window, select ANOVA: Single Factor. Screen W19.13 shows the Excel procedure. It is important that you include all the data when selecting the Input Range as shown in Screen W19.13.

Table W19.3 ───── ⎰⎱⎰⎱ Water Conservation Awareness Levels in Three Residential Areas

Area 1	Area 2	Area 3
5	8	6
6	7	3
2	9	5
5	5	7
8	6	8
9	7	5
10	7	7
4	8	4
5	6	3
7	8	
6		

Screen W19.13 ───── ⎰⎱⎰⎱ Excel Data Analysis ANOVA: Single Factor

The samples' descriptive statistics are presented in a Summary table and the results of the hypothesis test are included in an ANOVA table (see Screen W19.13). The null hypothesis of this test is that the three population means are the same and the alternate hypothesis is that they are different. The p-value (0.1298) of the F-test indicates that the difference is not statistically significant at the 5 percent level, which means that evidence is insufficient to indicate that the average awareness levels of the residents in the three areas are different.

REGRESSION

The Excel Data Analysis Regression procedure provides easy access to regression analysis. Let's look at an example of multiple regression to illustrate the procedure. The procedure for simple regression is the same. Environmental managers have long used environmental spending level, measured by environmental spending as a percentage of total government spending, to gauge a government's efforts in environmental protection and development. Environmental scientists speculate that this spending level is affected by population growth and economic activities. A regional planning agency has collected data on environmental spending, population densities, and manufacturing employment growth for 12 cities in the region (Table W19.4).

To use the Data Analysis Regression procedure, select the Data Analysis command in the Analysis group on the Data tab, and click Regression from the Data Analysis window. As shown in Screen W19.14, the dependent variable Y is the environmental spending level. The independent variable X range is the population density and manufacturing employment growth rate. Check the Labels box if you include variable names in your data ranges. Select an output range that does not overlap with the data.

The Excel Summary Output has three tables, also shown in Screen W19.14. The first table (Summary Output) provides R-square, adjusted R-square, and the standard error of the estimate. It also presents "multiple R," which is the correlation coefficient between the actual values and the predicted values of the dependent variable Y. The second table (ANOVA) presents the F-test result of the regression model. It shows that the model is statistically significant at the 10 percent level but not at the 5 percent level. The last table gives coefficients (unstandardized) of the independent variables and the constant (known as Intercept in Excel printout). In our example, the regression model is as follows: Environmental Spending Level = 0.0818 + 0.000235*Population Density + 0.0009175*Manufacturing Employment Growth Rate. The t-test results of slopes are also presented. The results show a possible positive impact of population density on environmental spending and that the relationship is statistically significant at the 5 percent ($p = .0452$). Nevertheless, there is no evidence of an impact of manufacturing growth on environmental spending ($p = .2833$). The output also presents 95 percent confidence intervals (as the default) for the estimates. You can specify the level of confidence interval estimates (for example, 99 percent).

Excel Data Analysis Regression also allows you to plot residuals against predicted values of the dependent variable as well as values of each independent variable in your effort to check the assumption of homoscedasticity. Screen W19.15 show the procedure to obtain the plot. The plot of residuals by the predicted values of the dependent variable in our environmental spending example is shown in Figure W19.1.

Table W19.4 ———〰〰— Data for a Multiple Regression

City ID	Environmental Spending (percentage of total spending)	Population Density (number of people per square mile)	Manufacturing Employment Growth Rate (past 5 years)
1	0.11	149	−11.0671
2	0.04	44	−5.33
3	0.26	459	13.0652
4	0.07	97	−28.0627
5	0.17	345	2.2198
6	0.13	523	−11.8397
7	0.08	24	−19.3277
8	0.22	275	3.8638
9	0.11	183	−16.0517
10	0.10	287	19.6831
11	0.20	137	11.3782
12	0.11	86	46.3274

Screen W19.14 ——— ∿ Excel Data Analysis Regression

Screen W19.15 ——— ∿ The Excel Procedure for Residual Plots in Regression

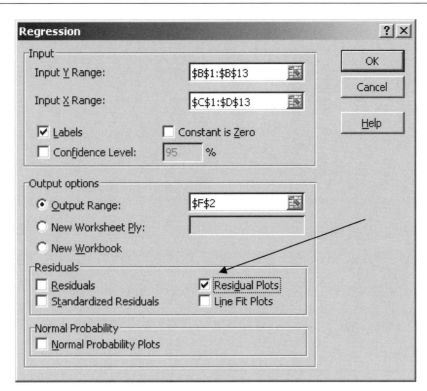

Figure 19.1 ——⋀⋀— The Plot of Residuals by Predicted Values

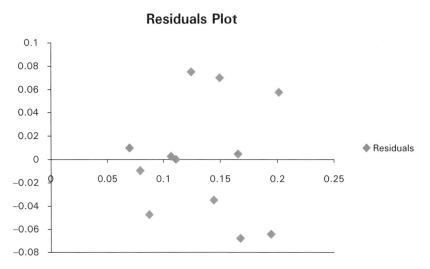

CREATING CHARTS IN EXCEL

Finally, we would like to introduce the Excel Chart function. It is very easy to create charts with Excel. You can do it by clicking the chart type in the Charts group on the Insert Tab of an Excel sheet. To create a professional-looking chart that displays the details that you want, you can modify the chart, apply predefined styles and layouts, and add various formatting features. For example, to create a line chart similar to the one in Figure 9.4 of the textbook, select the data for the presentation first, click the Line command in the Charts group on the Insert tab. (*Note:* If you use Excel 2003, click the Chart button on the Insert tab and you will be shown a list of chart types in the Chart Wizard window.) Select the Line with Markers on the Line tab. You should see a graph similar to that shown in Screen W19.16. Use the Design menu and the Layout menu to edit the graph.

Screen 19.16 ——⋀⋀— Creating an Excel Line Chart

CHAPTER
20

SPSS User's Guide

This chapter guides you through the operating characteristics of the Statistical Package for the Social Sciences (SPSS), now repacked by IBM as "PASW" or "IBM SPSS." This popular software is an invaluable tool for social scientists because of its capacity for handling large datasets and performing a wide range of statistical tests. Across many social science professions, including public administration and public policy analysis, SPSS software offers professionals, practitioners, and students alike the ability to perform myriad statistical procedures and data evaluation processes. Even better, it handles these analyses and operations without requiring users to perform intricate mathematical operations. Luckily, SPSS is also extremely easy to use. For those already familiar with various spreadsheet software programs, SPSS looks and feels quite similar. If you don't have previous experience with spreadsheets, there is no need for apprehension, since SPSS is truly user friendly. Through the initial familiarization exercises, you will quickly gain an appreciation of just how simple it is to use this software as a data analysis tool.

Of course, understanding the statistical concepts that underlie the tasks SPSS will perform is crucial. By analogy, if SPSS is viewed as a vehicle, then you are the driver and need to know the rules of the road. The textbook *Essential Statistics for Public Managers and Policy Analysts* is about the rules and practice of using statistics; studying it will help you develop a sense of what you need to look out for—such as data characteristics, causality patterns in relationships, and the assumptions and limitations of various statistical procedures. This chapter helps users get started with SPSS and shows them how to apply concepts discussed in the textbook. Enough said. Now, let's get started!

Note: Software versions change quickly these days, and perhaps some of the screen shots will be slightly different form your version. Still, we think the following will be helpful. as needed, you can always use the "Help→ Tutorial" that comes with your version for further answers and guidance, too. SPSS software is sold separately or as a bundle with this learning package.

SPSS SCREENS

After you open SPSS, the Data Editor screen will appear as shown in Screen W20.1. This screen will display the data, values, and labels for each dataset variable. Presently, no data are displayed because you have not yet created or opened a file in SPSS.

At the top of the screen is the toolbar from which SPSS commands are selected. These commands are the principal way of getting your data in shape for subsequent analysis. Note the Help function, which contains a tutorial to introduce you to the capabilities of SPSS. Investigating this tool is certainly worth the time investment and is highly recommended.

Take time to explore each of the toolbar menus and familiarize yourself with the options and functions of each. Don't worry if the terminology seems unfamiliar at first. As you progress through this guide, you will work your way through it.

At the bottom left of the SPSS Data Editor screen are two tabs, called Data View and Variable View. Select the Variable View tab. The screen displayed contains no information beyond the fields comprising that screen because no file has been opened yet. This screen will be explained and demonstrated when you create your first variable.

Screen W20.1 ───✛✛✛✛─── Data Editor Screen

To return to the Data View screen, merely select the tab at the bottom of the screen. SPSS also has an Output screen that will become familiar to you after you complete your first analysis.

CREATING A VARIABLE

Chapter 6 of the textbook uses sample data in the discussion of the mean, median, and mode. We will use those data to create your first variable and then see how easy it is for SPSS to perform statistical calculations. *Note:* Throughout this guide, the symbol → means "execute the next command immediately following the arrow." For example, Select Variable View → Name means "open the Variable View screen and then select Name by placing the cursor over the Name option and left clicking." Practice this command now.

To create the first variable, we will give it a name and a label. Go to the Variable View screen, and place the cursor in the first row of the cells in the Name column. In the first cell, type "variablx" as shown in Screen W20.2. We could have used a longer name than variablx, but variable names in SPSS have been limited historically to eight characters and many analysts still follow this practice. Variable names must start with a letter and may contain only letters and numbers, as well as periods when not used as the first or last character; thus, "variable x" is not a valid variable name (it contains an empty space), but "variablex" and "var.x" are. Don't worry about remembering what each variable name means; the purpose of the Label column is to fully define the variable name. We will show you how to create labels, too. (Once the label is entered, SPSS will use the label, rather than the variable name, in subsequent output tables.)

Entering the variable name automatically produces some additional settings, as shown in Screen W20.2. The next column allows selection of the type of variable. The default setting for Type is a numeric variable; your variable is numeric, since you will be entering numbers. To examine other options, highlight the cell in the first row of the Type column. This will bring up an icon in the right-hand sector of the data cell. When you click on that icon, you will see a pop-up menu, a typical feature of SPSS, from which you select the type of variable. In the case of variablx, select Numeric. This pop-up dialog box is shown in Screen W20.3. Continuing across, the first cell in the Width column identifies the maximum number of characters of this variable; the default is 8. The Decimals column indicates the number of decimals; the default is 2. Hence, the

Screen W20.2 ⟶⟶⟶ Naming Variables

default settings accommodate any value of variablx up to 99999.99. The Label column provides user-defined fields to further describe each variable. As shown in Screen W20.3, type in the label "Data for calculating mean, median and mode." (Double clicking on the Label data box allows label entry and editing of entries.) In later sections, you will learn more about the Values and Missing columns. The latter column is to the right of the screen, found by using the horizontal scroll bar at the bottom of the screen. The default for both is "None." The column labeled "Columns" adjusts the widths of the columns in the Data View screen. The widths of the columns in the Variable View screen can also be adjusted by placing the cursor between two columns until you see the icon that is used to adjust the widths of the columns, which looks like this:

On the right-hand side of the Variable View screen, you will see two additional columns. The Align column aligns the data in the Data View screen to the right, left, or center (this is somewhat analogous to the alignment of text in word processing programs). The rightmost column is labeled "Measure." Variables can be labeled as being nominal, ordinal, or scale (that is, continuous). This label is of no consequence in using most SPSS features later, nor does the label appear on most SPSS outputs. Rather, the label shows up on dialog boxes from which variables are selected, such as in Screen W20.5. This label may serve as a reminder to analysts of the measurement level of their variables. Here, we define variablx as a scale—the default label, which appears with a ruler icon to the left of the variable name in Screen W20.5. Many analysts ignore the option of labeling their measurement levels. Ordinal and nominal labels show up with other icons, namely, as bar charts and Venn diagrams (concentric circles), and an older, but still recent version of SPSS uses a "#" symbol (shown in Screen W20.11) for numeric variables. Again, these are just user-assigned labels that have no effect on our ability to use any statistical procedure later.

Return now to the Data View screen, where variablx is displayed. Place the cursor on variablx, and view the drop-down label defining the variable. The next step is to enter values for variablx. Enter the data from Chapter 6 in the textbook by selecting a data cell, entering a value, and then pressing Enter. (The data are also recorded by simply selecting the keyboard down arrow after entering the numeric data value in each cell.) In this manner, you should reproduce Screen W20.4. You have just completed the data entry for your first variable. Congratulations!

Screen W20.3 〜〜 Selecting Variable Type

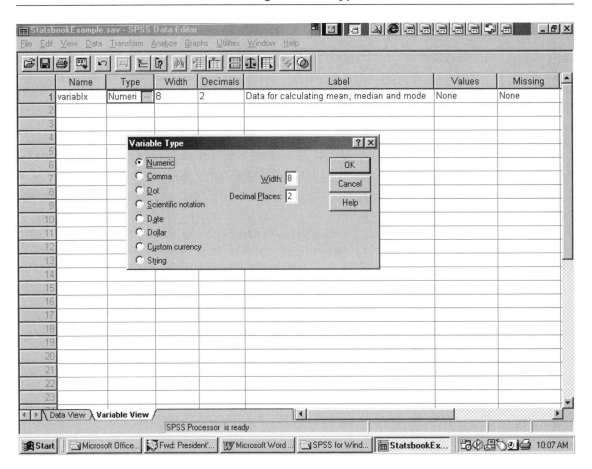

Screen W20.4 〜〜 Entering Data

UNIVARIATE ANALYSIS: MEANS AND FREQUENCY DISTRIBUTIONS

You are now ready to perform your first SPSS data analysis. From the toolbar, select Analyze → Descriptive Statistics → Frequencies, which produces the dialog box seen in Screen W20.5. Select variablx and then select the center arrow to move variablx to the Variable(s) box. Next, select the Statistics . . . button at the bottom of the dialog box. This action produces another dialog box, from which you can now select Mean, Median, and Mode, as shown by the checkmarks in Screen W20.6. Then select Continue.

You can also select other analyses. From the Frequency dialog box, select Charts . . . → Histograms → With normal curve, shown in Screen W20.7. Now select Continue to proceed.

After you return to the Frequencies screen, select OK in the Frequencies dialog box. SPSS will then perform the commands you just specified. Screen W20.8—called the Output screen (or Output Viewer)—will be produced. The scroll bar on the right-hand edge of the screen can be used to view the entire output.

Specifically, the results shown in Table W20.1 and Figure W20.1 are produced. (*Note:* You can cut and paste these results into a word processing program, which can be useful when preparing reports and slide shows. Table W20.1 and Figure W20.1 were reproduced in this way.) The number of bars is set by default. However, you can also adjust the number of bars shown in the histogram in Figure W20.1 by opening the Chart Editor. You can do this either by placing the cursor over the histogram on the Output screen and double clicking it, or by selecting Edit → SPSS Chart Object → Open. Once you see the Chart Editor dialog box, select Edit → Select X-Axis → Histogram Options: Bin Sizes → Custom. Select, for example, Number of intervals: 10, and then click Apply. Screen W20.9 shows how this selection changes the display.

If you had created a bar chart rather than a histogram, a separate bar would be created for each value of the variable. To create a bar chart, select Analyze → Descriptive Statistics → Frequencies → Charts: Bar charts. You might want to open up the Chart Editor, and then explore options for changing the bar chart.

Next, extend this example in the following way. The appendix to Chapter 7 in the textbook discusses how boxplots are used to determine whether individual observations are outliers. You might wonder

Screen W20.5 ————〰— Frequencies Dialog Box

Screen W20.6 ～√√～ Frequencies: Statistics Dialog Box

Screen W20.7 ～√√～ Creating a Histogram

Screen W20.8 ——————— Output Screen

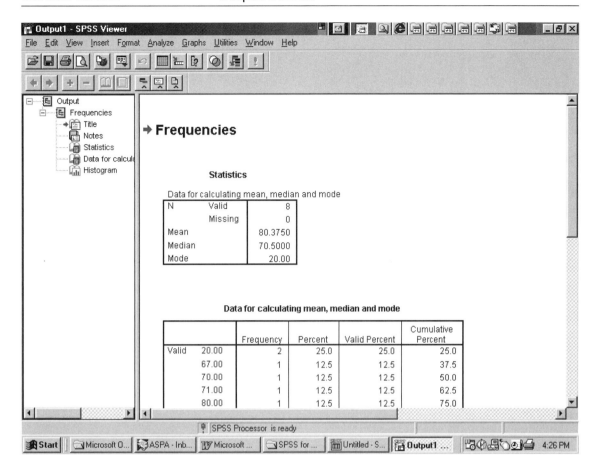

Table W20.1 ——————— SPSS Output (in Word Format)

Statistics VARIABLX		
N	Valid	8
	Missing	0
Mean		80.3750
Median		70.5000
Mode		20.00

VARIABLX	Frequency	Percent	Valid Percent	Cumulative Percent
Valid 20.00	2	25.0	25.0	25.0
67.00	1	12.5	12.5	37.5
70.00	1	12.5	12.5	50.0
71.00	1	12.5	12.5	62.5
80.00	1	12.5	12.5	75.0
90.00	1	12.5	12.5	87.5
225.00	1	12.5	12.5	100.0
Total	8	100.0	100.0	

whether the data point 225 is an outlier, as discussed in the textbook. SPSS can create a boxplot to find out. First, select from the toolbar Graphs → Boxplots. The dialog box shown in Screen W20.10 will appear.

Select Summaries of separate variables → Define. The dialog box shown in Screen W20.11 appears. Select the variable "variablx," and highlight the arrow to the left of the box labeled "Boxes Represent" so that you can drag the variable to the Boxes Represent box. Then, to continue, select OK. The output is produced

Figure W20.1 ———∿∿— Histogram

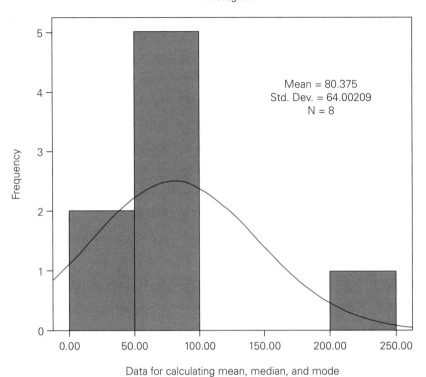

Data for calculating mean, median, and mode

Screen W20.9 ———∿∿— Chart Editor

in the Output screen, as shown in Screen W20.12. Examine the display. Notice that the X-axis depicts the number of cases as being "8." Also note that the eighth observation in the dataset is an outlier. As a part of examining a dataset, you should make a note of this observation because it may have an undue influence on further analyses. In this example, there are no observations with small values.

Screen W20.10 ⎯⎯⎯⎯ ᴧᴧ⎯ Boxplot Dialog Box

Screen W20.11 ⎯⎯⎯⎯ ᴧᴧ⎯ Defining Boxplot Variables

In SPSS, the same output can often be produced in different ways. For example, to produce the box-plot shown in Screen W20.12, you could have used Analyze → Explore → Variable: variablx → OK. No one way is better than any other; both result in the same output. Just choose whatever method works best for you.

To close the Output screen, select File → Close. At this point there is no need to save the output, so select No when asked if you would like to save it, and then return to the Data View screen. However, we will want to save this example dataset as "Example" because we will use it later to develop additional examples and SPSS demonstrations. To save the dataset, use File → Save As → File Name: Example → Save. Be sure to note the location of the saved file (for example, in a folder on a hard drive or on a portable memory device), so that you can find it again.

Screen W20.12 ——～⋀～—— Boxplot Output Screen

VARIABLE LABELS AND VALUES

Open the Public Perceptions dataset, which can be found on the CD that accompanies this workbook, and be sure you are in the Data View screen. SPSS can show the data both as numbers and as value labels. If you see all labels, as in Screen W20.13, you might want to see the coded numbers instead. To do so, select View → Value Labels. When you see value labels, the Value Labels option has been selected, as shown in Screen W20.13. (Note the check mark next to Value Labels.) To view numbers, simply click on Value Labels to switch off this option (the check mark will disappear). Then the fields will show numbers.

Screen W20.13 ——～⋀～—— Value Labels

Screen W20.14 ———〜〜〜— Value Labels Dialog Box

You can also view the value labels in the Variable View screen. In the Variable View screen, select the cell in the Values column that corresponds, for example, with the variable "control." Click on that cell and double click on the square icon that appears in the cell, which will generate the dialog box shown in Screen W20.14. This box defines the values that correspond with the labels "Very Important," "Important," "Somewhat Important," and "Unimportant." Often, you will want to assign values to a variable. For example, on a scale of 1–4, a 1 might indicate that a respondent is "very satisfied" regarding some survey question. Such labels later appear on your output, as well, greatly improving presentation.

Note: Students using the *Public Perceptions—Exercising Essential Statistics* dataset created for use with the *SPSS Student Version* software will notice a slight difference with regard to screen W20.13: row 23 will show the variable "busneeds" rather than "arts." This difference reflects the omission of some variables (such as "pubsafe") from the full Public Perceptions dataset in order to accommodate the restrictions of the *SPSS Student Version* software described on the accompanying CD. However, none of these omitted variables are relevant to any material in this workbook, including this chapter.

Now you should practice generating value labels on the Example dataset you saved earlier. Assigning labels is quite simple. Open the Example dataset. The screen shown in Screen W20.15 should be displayed. Select the Variable View screen. First, create a new variable with which you will practice. In row 2 of the Name column, type "dataskil," which is the name of your variable, shown in Screen W20.16. In the Label column, type "Importance of data analysis skills." This variable represents a hypothetical question posed to public sector managers concerning the importance of data analysis skills. (Double clicking on the Label data box allows label entry and editing of entries.)

Now define data values. Select the box in the Values column data cell for the variable "dataskil." Enter "1" in the Value box and then "Very Important" in the Value Label box. The dialog box should now look as in Screen W20.16. Select Add. This causes the definition to be entered into SPSS programming. After you select Add, Screen W20.17 should appear. Repeat this process. Define the scale values "Important," "Somewhat Important," and Unimportant," which results in Screen W20.18. Select OK to complete the value definitions for this variable. All that remains is for the researcher to enter the data for this hypothetical question.

Screen W20.15 ———— ⌁ —— Generating Labels

Screen W20.16 ———— ⌁ —— Defining Data Values

Screen W20.17 ———— ⌇⌇ ———— Adding Labels

Screen W20.18 ———— ⌇⌇ ———— Value Label Definitions

DEFINING MISSING VALUES

A common problem is the coding and handling of missing values. Missing values are blank cells in the Data View screen when an observation has a missing value for a specific variable. Sometimes, however, analysts want to assign a specific value for missing values. Doing so helps differentiate between a value that an analyst has forgotten to enter and a value that really is missing, which occurs when a respondent does not answer a particular question. Suppose you wish to assign the value of "9" as our way of coding missing values. Select the Variable View screen, and highlight the cell in the second row of the "Missing" column. Screen W20.19 will be displayed. Next, select Discrete missing values, and enter a "9" in the first block, and then select OK. This will cause every "9" for the given variable (in this case, dataskil) to be treated as missing. Proper definition of missing data is extremely important to ensure accurate data analysis.

Screen W20.20 shows another highly useful feature of SPSS. Variable definitions (for example, missing values, data values, or labels) are readily copied from one variable to a range of other variables. Thus, you need to define missing values and data values (labels) only once. Indeed, after you create more new variables, newvar1 through newvar5, as shown in Screen W20.20, simply copy and paste the Values definition of the variable "dataskil" to these new cells. You do not need to define these values for each new variable. Similarly, you can now copy and paste the missing values definition from the variable "dataskil" to these new variables, too.

SELECTING A SUBSET OF OBSERVATIONS FOR ANALYSIS

Often, analysts want to perform their analyses on a subset of observations. Using the Public Perceptions dataset, assume that you wish to assess perceptions of client satisfaction, but *only* among those respondents who have had contact with a county employee during the past year. Then, you would want to select for subsequent analysis only those observations that meet this condition.

Open the Public Perceptions dataset. The variable "contact" (row 29) measures whether the respondent has had contact with county employees within the past year. To filter out respondents not meeting this criterion, perform the following sequence of commands. From the toolbar, select Data → Select Cases → If condition is satisfied. Add "contact" to the right-hand box, and type "=1". Screen W20.21 is displayed. Select Continue → OK.

Screen W20.19 ——— Missing Values Dialog Box

Screen W20.20 ——— ∿∿— Copying Variable Definitions

Screen W20.21 ——— ∿∿— Selecting Cases (Filtering Observations)

Screen W20.22 —⋀⋁— Selected Cases

	case	control	cuttax	eyefour	mass	ltrail	roadcond	roadapp	contgrow	protenv
1	1	2	1	1	3	3	1	3	3	3
2	2	3	3	3	3	3	3	3	3	3
3	3	3	3	3	1	3	1	3	3	3
4	4	1	3	3	1	1	1	0	2	2
5	5	2	2	3	3	3	3	3	1	2
6	6	3	3	3	2	1	3	1	2	3
7	7	2	3	1	3	0	3	2	0	2
8	8	3	1	2	0	1	2	1	0	2
9	9	3	3	2	0	0	0	2	3	3
10	10	3	1	2	0	0	3	3	0	0
11	11	3	2	2	2	2	2	1	3	3
12	12	2	0	3	2	0	3	0	2	3
13	13	3	0	3	0	0	3	3	1	1
14	14	3	1	2	2	1	2	1	2	2
15	15	3	3	3	3	2	2	2	2	3
16	16	2	2	2	2	0	2	2	2	2
17	17	3	2	3	3	2	2	2	2	3
18	18	3	2	3	2	3	2	1	2	3
19	19	3	3	3	3	2	3	3	2	3
20	20	3	1	3	1	0	2	1	2	1
21	21	0	2	3	2	0	3	0	2	2
22	22	3	3	3	3	0	3	3	3	3

Note the left-hand column of the Data View screen. Observations not meeting our new requirement of having contact with county employees during the past year now show a diagonal line through their respective sequence number, indicating that they are not included in subsequent calculations (Screen W20.22). (To undo this restriction, simply choose Data → Select Cases → Select: All cases → OK.)

INDEX VARIABLES I: CRONBACH ALPHA

Chapter 3 of the textbook discusses the use of index variables to measure concepts comprised of several dimensions. In short, different variables are used to measure different dimensions, and these variables are subsequently aggregated into an index variable.

Remember, index variable construction is a two-step process. Before aggregating the data, you need to *justify* (that is, to persuasively argue) that the disparate variables indeed measure different dimensions of the same underlying concept (see Chapter 3 of the textbook). The justification should be based on theoretical grounds (do the variables make sense as dimensions of the same underlying concept?) and empirical grounds. One way to empirically justify the selection of variables is to examine the extent to which the disparate variables are correlated with each other. If the variables measure dimensions of the *same* concept, then the dimensions should be correlated with each other, as well.

Cronbach alpha is the measure that assesses the empirical correlation (or internal reliability) of variables. As discussed in Chapter 3, values between 0.80 and 1.00 indicate high internal reliability, and values between 0.70 and 0.80 indicate moderate but acceptable internal reliability.

Open the Public Perceptions dataset. This dataset contains several variables (survey items) that can be used to measure customer satisfaction. Specifically, go to the Variable View screen. Scroll down to the first of these variables, helpful (on or about row 32). Double click on the Label cell; this allows you to scroll the entire label entry ("the employees were helpful"). The other variables—respect, friendly, nomistak, timely, and exceed—are immediately below that variable. These individual variables appear to be possible dimensions of an overall concept, for example, "customer satisfaction." Screen W20.23 also shows the value labels for these items (rows 32 through 37).

Next, examine the Cronbach alpha statistic to determine whether these items are adequately correlated with each other. But first, practice what you learned in the previous section; you wish to create the index variable only for respondents who have had contact with county officials in the past year. Select only those observations that meet this condition, that is, "contact=1." This selection produces a screen similar to Screen W20.21.

The command sequence for producing the Cronbach alpha statistic is Analyze → Scale → Reliability Analysis. Add all six variables to the Items box. Then, select Statistics and, from the "Descriptives for" box, the items "Item," "Scale," "Scale if item deleted," as shown in Screen W20.24. Then, to perform the analysis, select Continue and OK. Screen W20.25 shows the results. Note that the value for alpha is .8825. This value is well within the required range of 0.8 to 1.0, indicating a very high degree of *internal consistency* (or *internal reliability*). Also note that deleting any item (variable), as shown in the right-hand column, results in a lower value for alpha. Therefore, combining these separate dimension variables into a concept index variable, "customer satisfaction," is empirically justified. Finally, note that the number of observations is now limited to 353, reflecting both the constraint (contact=1) and missing values for some of the six variables. (If the analysis had not been limited to only those respondents who have had contact, the result would have been $n = 615$ and alpha = .8855, resulting in the same conclusion.)

Screen W20.23 ——— Value Labels for Public Perceptions Dataset

Screen W20.24 ———— Producing Cronbach Alpha

Screen W20.25 ———— Cronbach Alpha Output

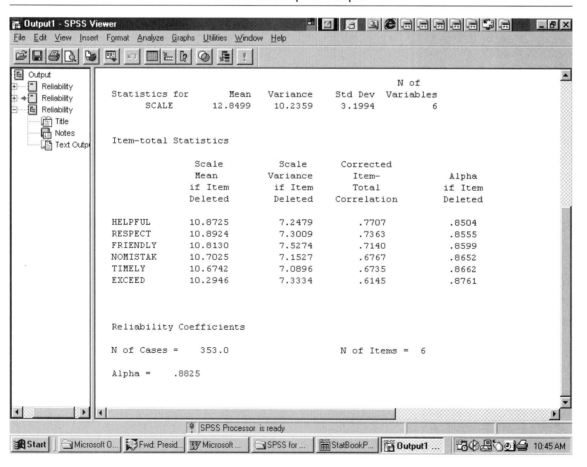

INDEX VARIABLES II: CONSTRUCTION

Now you will construct the index variable. From the toolbar, select Transform → Compute. The Compute Variable dialog box will appear (Screen W20.26). In the Target Variable box, enter the name of your new index variable for customer satisfaction, satisfyd. In the Numeric Expression box, enter the six variables comprising your index variable, and divide by six. Be sure to note the brackets in Screen W20.25 to ensure the appropriate division. Then select OK. Examine the Data View screen; satisfyd is now the last variable. Examine the new variable using Analyze → Descriptive Statistics → Frequencies, which yields the results shown in Screen W20.27. Also, you can produce summary statistics by selecting Frequencies → Statistics; choose Mean, Median, and Mode from the Central Tendency box, and then select Continue → OK.

RECODING DATA

Depending on a variable's data distribution, there may be so many response categories and resulting low frequency counts that recoding the variable is not only appropriate but will also allow for more meaningful data interpretation. Redefining data into new categories is a relatively simple process.

Open the Public Perceptions dataset. Perform a frequency distribution and histogram of the variable "ethnic." The output shown in Screen W20.28 and Figure W20.2 is produced. (Be sure to select all cases for this analysis.) You will see that "ethnic" has several response categories with low counts. Asian/Pacific Islander (category 4), Native American (5), and Other (6) could be reasonably redefined as an aggregate variable "Other." Doing so would yield a total of four categories within the variable "ethnic." Specifically, the new variable, "ethrecod," will have the following categories: 1 = White, 2 = Black/African-American, 3 = Hispanic, and 4 = Other.

Screen W20.26 ───────\\/\\/\\/─── Constructing the Index Variable for "Customer Satisfaction"

Screen W20.27 ———— ⎍⎍⎍— Output Screen for Satisfyd

Screen W20.28 ———— ⎍⎍⎍— Output Screen for Ethnic

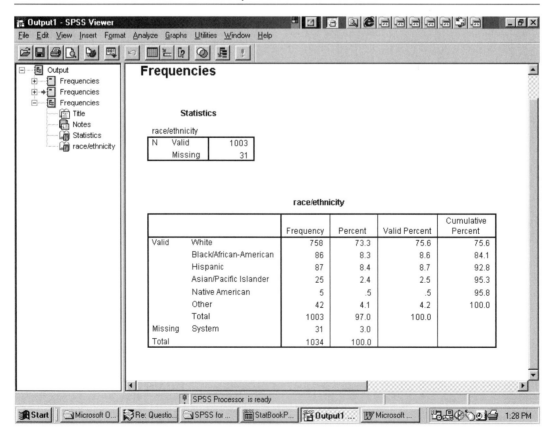

Figure W20.2 ━━━━━∿∿━ Race/Ethnicity Output

race/ethnicity

To perform recoding, you will recode and create a new variable, "ethrecod," in order to preserve the coding of the existing variable. Select Transform → Recode → Into Different Variables. Then select the existing variable, "ethnic," which results in the dialog box shown in Screen W20.29. Note that the dialog box is now prompting the user for the name of the new variable (note the question mark in the dialog box). Type "ethrecod" in the Name box, shown in Screen W20.30. Next, select Change (in the far right of the dialog box) to complete this part of the variable recoding, which should produce Screen W20.31.

Now that you have defined the new variable, you must define the new categories. Select Old and New Values, which brings up the dialog box shown in Screen W20.32. The original values for response categories 1 should be retained. Enter "1" for both Old Value and New Value, and then Add. In turn, Screens W20.33 and W20.34 are produced.

Screen W20.29 ━━━━━∿∿━ Recoding Values for Ethnic

Screen W20.30 ———— ᶺᵕᵕ— Naming the Variable

Screen W20.31 ———— ᶺᵕᵕ— Recoding Dialog Box

Screen W20.32 ───── ∿∿ Old and New Values

Screen W20.33 ───── ∿∿ Entering New Value

Screen W20.34 ⎯⎯⎯⎯⎯~⋀~⎯ Old to New Values

Continue this procedure for response categories 2 and 3. Now recode response categories 4, 5, and 6 into a single new category, 4. Select Range, and enter "4" and "6". Note that the New Value cell is now illuminated; enter "4" → Add. To ensure that missing data from the original variable are retained and recognized as such by SPSS, select "System- or user-missing" under Old Value, and "System-missing" under New Value → Add. Screen W20.35 is displayed. As an important side note, observe the two cells "System- or user-missing" and "System-missing." System-missing cells are empty, whereas user-missing cells have user-defined missing values, as discussed earlier. It is a safe practice to specify System- or user-missing when the intent is to refer to all missing values. In this case, the Public Perceptions dataset does not contain user-defined missing values (verify this in the Variable View screen, Missing column); thus, using System-missing and System- or user-missing produces the same result.

Select Continue and OK to complete the recoding. To verify that the recoding was successful, perform a Frequency Distribution (recall, Analyze → Descriptive Statistics → Frequencies). The output shown in Screen W20.36 and Figure W20.3 are displayed. The total number of valid responses is still 1,003; there are still 31 missing system values; and the total number of responses is still 1,034. Also, the number of responses comprising the new value of 4 is 72, the sum of Old Values (prior to recoding) of categories 4, 5, and 6. To finish construction of the new variable, "ethrecod," remember to define Values and Label on the Variable View screen.

The same procedure is used to define a response value *within* a variable as missing. For example, from the Public Perceptions dataset, select the variable "trust." This variable has three response categories, "Yes," "No," and "Can't Say." To recode "Can't Say" as a missing value, select Transform → Recode → Into Same Variable. When defining response category 3, enter "3" under Old Value and then select "System-missing" for the New Value. The dialog box shown in Screen W20.37 should be displayed. Select Continue to complete the recoding. Examine the variable "trust." Previous cells containing a "Can't Say" response are now coded as missing, as indicated by a period.

Screen W20.35 ⎯⎯⎯⎯⎯⎯⎯⎯⎯⎯ Missing Data Screen

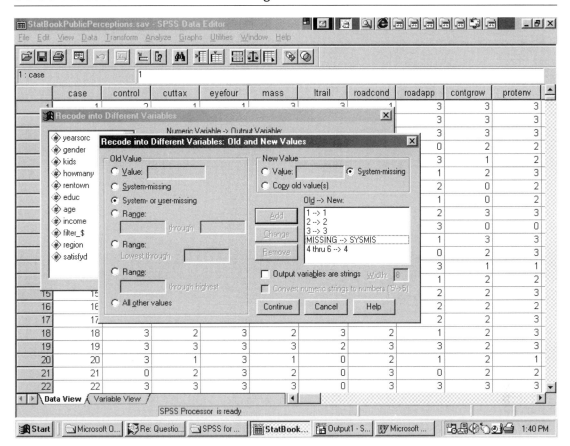

Screen W20.36 ⎯⎯⎯⎯⎯⎯⎯⎯⎯⎯ Output for Recoded Data

Figure W20.3 ———————— Recoded Data Bar Chart

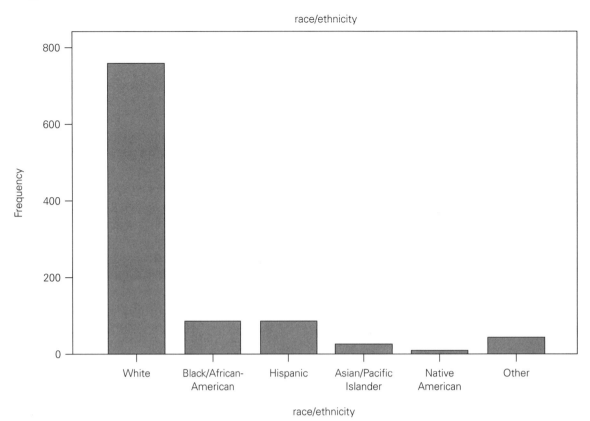

Screen W20.37 ———————— Recoding Response as a Missing Category

Another use for recoding might be to combine response categories from scales, possibly when cell counts are less than sufficient for evaluation. For example, a seven-point Likert scale might have the following response categories: "Strongly Agree," "Agree," "Somewhat Agree," "Neutral," "Somewhat Disagree," "Disagree," and "Strongly Disagree." This scale could be easily recoded to five response categories by recoding "Strongly Agree/Agree" to "Agree," and "Strongly Disagree/Disagree" to "Disagree."

HYPOTHESIS TESTING WITH CHI-SQUARE

In Chapter 8 of the textbook, you learned that a *contingency table* expresses the relationship between two categorical variables. One variable is shown in rows and the other in columns. Each row shows the frequency of observations with specific values for both variables. Typically, column totals are present. Statistics such as chi-square express the relationship between variables quantitatively. SPSS easily performs contingency table analysis.

Open the Public Perceptions dataset. In the Variable View screen, highlight the variable "interest." The variable label identifies that this variable assesses the extent to which respondents feel county government is interested in what they have to say about issues affecting them. An analyst might ask whether a significant difference exists between the opinions held by male and female respondents on this question.

Chapter 10 of the textbook discusses the concept of the null hypothesis and its application in hypothesis testing. For this exercise, the null hypothesis (H_0) is "Gender has no effect on perception of government interest in citizen opinions." The alternative hypothesis (H_A) is "Gender does influence perceptions of government interest in citizen opinions." You now want to examine whether sufficient statistical evidence exists to reject the null hypothesis and, hence, establish that a relationship does exist. To test this hypothesis, select Analyze → Descriptive Statistics → Crosstabs. Then select "gender" in the column and "interest" in rows. Also, select Statistics → Chi-square → Continue. The dialog box shown in Screen W20.38 will be displayed. Note how the selection of "gender" in the column is consistent with Chapter 10 in the textbook.

Next, select Cells → Observed → Column → Total → Continue → OK. The results in Figure W20.4 will be produced. First, note that 443 males and 551 females make up the total sample. Second, note the

Screen W20.38 ⎯⎯⎯ᴧᴧᴧ⎯ Chi-Square Dialog Box

Figure W20.4 ⎯⎯〰⎯ Chi-Square Output

I believe that the county government is interested in what I have to say about issues that affect me.
*gender Crosstabulation

			gender		Total
			male	female	
I believe that the county government is interested in what I have to say about issues that affect me.	Strongly Agree	Count	11	19	30
		% within gender	2.5%	3.4%	3.0%
	Agree	Count	236	326	562
		% within gender	53.3%	59.2%	56.5%
	Disagree	Count	153	171	324
		% within gender	34.5%	31.0%	32.6%
	Strongly Disagree	Count	43	35	78
		% within gender	9.7%	6.4%	7.8%
Total		Count	443	551	994
		% within gender	100.0%	100.0%	100.0%

Chi-Square Tests

	Value	df	Asymp. Sig. (2-sided)
Pearson Chi-Square	6.711[a]	3	.082
Likelihood Ratio	6.699	3	.082
Linear-by-Linear Association	6.590	1	.010
N of Valid Cases	944		

a. 0 cells (.0%) have expected count less than 5. The minimum expected count is 13.37

percentages produced within columns. These indicate how males and females responded to this question. For example, 34.5 percent of males and 31.0 percent of females disagree that county government is interested in what they have to say about issues affecting them.

Review the remaining response categories. Is there a significant difference between male and female respondents? To answer that question, you should rely on the chi-square calculation, which produces the results also shown in Figure W20.4. The chi-square value 6.711 is significant at the 0.082 level. Since this value exceeds the 0.05 standard for statistical significance, you cannot reject the null hypothesis, which means that there is insufficient statistical evidence to conclude that a relationship exists between gender and interest shown by county officials in issues that affect respondents.

T-TESTS

Chapter 12 of the textbook discusses how t-tests are used to determine whether two groups have different means of a continuous variable. For example, do men and women differ in their opinion of the quality of service they receive from county employees? If there is a perceived difference, perhaps county employees deal differently with male and female residents. Again, you need to limit the analysis to those respondents who have had contact with county employees (that is, if contact = 1; see "Selecting a Subset of Observations for Analysis," above).

The null hypothesis (H_0) in this case is "Men and women do not have different opinions of the quality of service they receive from county employees." The alternate hypothesis (H_A) is "Men and women do have different opinions of the quality of service they receive from county employees."

Open the Public Perceptions dataset. Select Analyze → Compare Means → Independent Samples T-Test. Screen W20.39 will be displayed. Enter "satisfyd" in the Test Variable box and gender in the Grouping Variable box. SPSS requires definition of the dichotomous values of "gender" that constitute the grouping variable. Enter "1" and "2" for Group 1 and Group 2, respectively. (When the grouping variable is continuous, a cutoff point—called "Cut point" in Screen W20.40—is specified, which creates the two groups.)

Screen W20.39 ———〜〜〜— Output Screen for T-Test

Screen W20.40 ———〜〜〜— Independent Samples T-Test Dialog Box

Screen W20.41 ──∿∿── Output Screen for T-Test

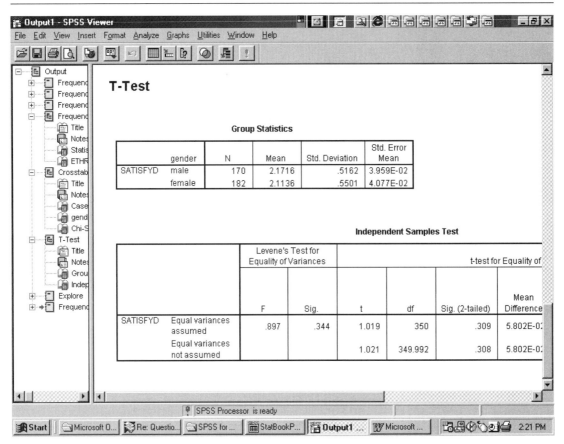

Select Continue → OK. The output shown in Screen W20.41 is produced. The results show that the mean level of satisfaction is 2.17 among men and 2.11 among women. The statistical question is whether this difference in the survey sample is large enough to suggest that a difference exists in the population of all county residents, as well.

As discussed in Chapter 12 of the textbook, using a t-test is a two-step process. First, we test whether the variances of the two groups are equal. The null hypothesis is that variances are equal. According to the output shown in Screen W20.41, you cannot reject this null hypothesis ($p = .344$). Second, you will test whether the difference of means (2.17 versus 2.11) is statistically significant. The result of this t-test is 1.019, which is significant at $p = .309$. This value exceeds the standard of 5 percent; thus, you conclude that in the population of all county residents, no statistically significant difference exists between men and women with regard to this item. (You also could have examined certain assumptions of the t-test, such as whether the variable is normally distributed and whether any extreme values are present that might affect the analysis.)

CONCLUSION

By now, you have seen just how valuable a tool statistical software can be to public managers and policy analysts. In particular, SPSS's user-friendly package can make statistics easier and save valuable time by "doing the math." Instead of struggling through cumbersome equations, analysts can quickly assess their data and present their findings. In short, analysts now readily recognize the importance of statistical software packages such as SPSS in helping them to quickly add value to decision-making processes.

This guide touched on a number of practical statistical applications, but SPSS has many other features, which you can explore on your own. For example, SPSS can be used to merge datasets, which is described on the accompanying CD (see "SPSS Student Version"). SPSS can also produce a wide range of other statistics. After you have familiarized yourself with other statistics described in the textbook, be sure to consult the SPSS manual that comes with your software to learn about other software features and functions.

Dataset Documentation

PUBLIC PERCEPTIONS

General Description

The Public Perceptions dataset includes data from 1,034 telephone interviews among residents of Orange County, Florida. Orange County is the central metropolitan county of Central Florida, encompassing many major tourist attractions. Random digit dialing was used to select interviewees. This is a general citizen survey, encompassing assessments of general county conditions, satisfaction with county services, and demographic items.

As students, some of you may wonder why you should care about these results from Florida. The answer is simple: they could very well have been from your city or county. Such general surveys help managers and policy makers know, in valid ways, where citizens stand on a broad range of issues. Moreover, many citizen surveys explore related questions, and you may be involved in a similar effort or one that is targeted at assessing perceptions about a specific program or service.

Methods

A full description of the survey methods used to develop this dataset is provided in Box 5.2 of the textbook.

Detailed Summary

The survey instrument has seven sections encompassing 96 separate items and is reproduced below. The first section asks the importance of various issues to residents, from controlling government spending to building a light rail transportation system. The rationale for asking these questions is that their ranking may inform county officials in their strategic planning and allocation decisions. The second section asks about perceptions of service experience, generally. Customer service is a key concern to jurisdictions, especially those located close to Disney World, which offers world-class customer service. The third section assesses overall satisfaction with selected county services. The fourth section asks about property taxes. The fifth section addresses a few wide-ranging questions on some matters of current interest to the county. Of particular interest was how often residents watched the local county cable TV station, called Orange TV. The sixth section addresses some general conditions, such as trust in government, expectations of living in Orange County in future years, and perceptions of race relations. Finally, the seventh section provides demographic data regarding age, gender, income, race, and other items. These items are relevant to the analysis of the preceding items. For example, are overall levels of satisfaction with Orange County services associated with perceptions of public safety?

Note on Variables

Each survey item is represented as a variable in the dataset. The variables appear in the same order as in the survey instrument. The variable names are limited to eight characters, and the labels are consistent with the survey items. Variable values are indicated on the survey below, in the first line of each section or as appropriate. Missing values have been coded as periods (.) in the dataset. The sections use a broad range of response scales. The scale on the first section is modified from a seven-point Likert scale. Because all of these items were thought to be of some importance to respondents, a decision was made to group the categories "Very Unimportant," "Unimportant," and "Somewhat Unimportant" in one category labeled "Unimportant."

The survey also includes one continuous variable, the index variable "satisfac." This variable is the average of the six items shown in Survey Question II, which assesses citizen contact with county employees. This variable is provided only for the 353 respondents who have had contact.

Students using *SPSS Student Version* software will find additional information relevant to that software on the CD that accompanies this workbook.

Survey Instrument: Orange County Citizen Survey

Hi, My name is _____, and I'm calling from the Survey Research Laboratory at the University of Central Florida. This is a legitimate survey; I'm not selling anything. We want to know how you feel about several issues facing Orange County. Of course, your participation is completely voluntary, but we hope you will participate. The entire interview should take less than ten minutes. The validity of our results depends on your willingness to help, so we hope that you will participate. Of course, you may discontinue the interview at any time or refuse to answer any questions that make you uncomfortable. We will only report group tendencies in this survey. Your individual answers will be held in strict confidence. Do you have any questions you want to ask before we begin? If you have any questions after the survey, you should call _____, at UCF. His number is 407-xxx-xxxx.

In order for our survey to be valid, we must interview only persons over the age of eighteen living in Orange County. Would that be you?

If "NO," ask to speak to someone who is eligible, and start over or terminate the call.

I.   How important are the following issues for you? Please state whether you consider each issue Very Important, Important, Somewhat Important, or Unimportant:

	Very Important	Important	Somewhat Important	Unimportant
Controlling government spending	[3]	[2]	[1]	[0]
Cutting property taxes	[ ]	[ ]	[ ]	[ ]
Reducing I-4 congestion	[ ]	[ ]	[ ]	[ ]
Improving mass transit	[ ]	[ ]	[ ]	[ ]
Building light rail	[ ]	[ ]	[ ]	[ ]
The condition of roadway system	[ ]	[ ]	[ ]	[ ]
Improving the appearance of roadways, such as by burying overhead power lines, reducing the number of billboards, and adding greenery	[ ]	[ ]	[ ]	[ ]
Controlling development and growth	[ ]	[ ]	[ ]	[ ]
Protecting environmentally sensitive land	[ ]	[ ]	[ ]	[ ]
Fighting against illegal drug use	[ ]	[ ]	[ ]	[ ]
Addressing problem of gangs and gang violence, including removing graffiti	[ ]	[ ]	[ ]	[ ]
Increasing code enforcement, such as removing junk and abandoned cars from neighborhoods	[ ]	[ ]	[ ]	[ ]
Helping public schools	[ ]	[ ]	[ ]	[ ]
Providing youth improvement programs, including after-school programs	[ ]	[ ]	[ ]	[ ]

	Very Important	Important	Somewhat Important	Unimportant
Providing better job training in Orange County	[ ]	[ ]	[ ]	[ ]
Increasing public safety, including hiring more deputies	[ ]	[ ]	[ ]	[ ]
Providing better storm water drainage	[ ]	[ ]	[ ]	[ ]
Improving the water quality of lakes	[ ]	[ ]	[ ]	[ ]
Promoting welfare to work programs	[ ]	[ ]	[ ]	[ ]
Promoting high tech jobs in Central Florida	[ ]	[ ]	[ ]	[ ]
Reducing discrimination	[ ]	[ ]	[ ]	[ ]
Promoting the arts in Central Florida	[ ]	[ ]	[ ]	[ ]
Addressing the needs of business	[ ]	[ ]	[ ]	[ ]
Addressing the needs of senior citizens through programs and services	[ ]	[ ]	[ ]	[ ]
Helping neighborhoods	[ ]	[ ]	[ ]	[ ]
Improving the parks	[ ]	[ ]	[ ]	[ ]
Increasing the level of wages	[ ]	[ ]	[ ]	[ ]

II. Have you had contact with any Orange County employees during the past twelve months (not a family member or friend)?

Yes [1]   No [2]

If yes, was this: by phone [1], face-to-face [2], or both [3]? *(Check one.)*
On the average, how often do you visit county offices?_____ (number)

Thinking about those experiences, or your most recent contact with a County employee, please tell me whether you Strongly Agree, Agree, Disagree, or Strongly Disagree with the following statements:

	Strongly Agree	Agree	Disagree	Strongly Disagree
The employees were helpful.	[1]	[2]	[3]	[4]
The employees treated me with courtesy and respect.	[ ]	[ ]	[ ]	[ ]
The employees were friendly.	[ ]	[ ]	[ ]	[ ]
The service was provided without mistakes.	[ ]	[ ]	[ ]	[ ]
The service experience exceeded my expectations.	[ ]	[ ]	[ ]	[ ]
The service was provided in a timely manner.	[ ]	[ ]	[ ]	[ ]

III. How satisfied are you with the following services in Orange County? Would you say you are
      Very Satisfied, Satisfied, Dissatisfied, or Very Dissatisfied?

	Very Satisfied	Satisfied	Don't Know	Dissatisfied	Very Dissatisfied
Law enforcement	[1]	[2]	[3]	[4]	[5]
Fire and rescue services	[ ]	[ ]	[ ]	[ ]	[ ]
The condition of road pavement	[ ]	[ ]	[ ]	[ ]	[ ]
Water	[ ]	[ ]	[ ]	[ ]	[ ]
Sewer	[ ]	[ ]	[ ]	[ ]	[ ]
Parks and recreation	[ ]	[ ]	[ ]	[ ]	[ ]
Code enforcement	[ ]	[ ]	[ ]	[ ]	[ ]
Orange TV	[ ]	[ ]	[ ]	[ ]	[ ]
Orange County Internet homepage	[ ]	[ ]	[ ]	[ ]	[ ]
Roadway system	[ ]	[ ]	[ ]	[ ]	[ ]
Schools	[ ]	[ ]	[ ]	[ ]	[ ]
The current level of county taxes and fees	[ ]	[ ]	[ ]	[ ]	[ ]
County jail	[ ]	[ ]	[ ]	[ ]	[ ]

IV. Do you think county property taxes are:

Too high	[1]
Too low	[2]
Just about right	[3]
Don't know	[4]

V.   The following questions can be answered with a simple yes or no.

Do you trust Orange County Government to do what is right most of the time?
  Yes [1]   No [2]   Can't Say [3]

Do you believe that Orange County Government works efficiently?
  Yes [ ]   No [ ]   Can't Say [ ]

Has Orange County done a good job of balancing growth against
environmental concerns?
  Yes [ ]   No [ ]   Can't Say [ ]

Is your household better off financially than one year ago?
  Yes [ ]   No [ ]   Can't Say [ ]

Has Orange County Government done a good job of managing growth?
  Yes [ ]   No [ ]   Can't Say [ ]

Do you watch Orange TV?
  Yes [ ]   No [ ]   Can't Say [ ]

Have you watched Board of County Commission meetings on Orange TV
during the last twelve months?
  Yes [ ]   No [ ]   Can't Say [ ]

Have you ever attended a Board of County Commission meeting?
  Yes [ ]   No [ ]   Can't Say [ ]

VI. I will read you some statements. Please tell me whether you Strongly Agree, Agree, Disagree, or Strongly Disagree with the following statements.

	Strongly Agree	Agree	Disagree	Strongly Disagree
I believe that the county government is interested in what I have to say about issues that affect me.	[1]	[2]	[3]	[4]
I know what services the county provides.	[ ]	[ ]	[ ]	[ ]
I rarely contact the county government.	[ ]	[ ]	[ ]	[ ]
The media accurately present county government issues.	[ ]	[ ]	[ ]	[ ]
I have a positive view of Orange County Government.	[ ]	[ ]	[ ]	[ ]
I feel comfortable voicing my opinions to county officials.	[ ]	[ ]	[ ]	[ ]
People in my neighborhood work together to solve their problems.	[ ]	[ ]	[ ]	[ ]
Local schools are doing a good job.	[ ]	[ ]	[ ]	[ ]
Race relations are good in Orange County.	[ ]	[ ]	[ ]	[ ]
I expect economic conditions in Orange County to improve.	[ ]	[ ]	[ ]	[ ]
The economic future looks bright for my household.	[ ]	[ ]	[ ]	[ ]
The quality of life in Orange County is good.	[ ]	[ ]	[ ]	[ ]
I expect the quality of life in Orange County to improve.	[ ]	[ ]	[ ]	[ ]
I expect to be living in Orange County five years from now.	[ ]	[ ]	[ ]	[ ]

VII. Your answers to the following questions will help us better analyze the results of this survey. Let me remind you that you may skip any question you choose not to answer.

What is the zip code of your residence? _____ (number)

   Note: The dataset includes the variable "region," which is based on this item.

How long have you lived in Orange County? _____ (number) years

What is your gender? Male [1] Female [2]

Do you have children under eighteen years old living at home with you?

                          Yes [1] No [2]

If Yes: How many? _____ (number)

Do you rent or own your home?   Rent [1]   Own [2]   Other [3]

How much formal schooling have you had?   Less than HS   [1]
                                                  High School   [2]
                                                  Some College   [3]
                                                  College Graduate [4]
                       Graduate or Professional Degree   [5]

What is your age? 18–24   [1]
                                                           25–35   [2]
                                                           36–45   [3]
                                                           46–55   [4]
                                                           56–65   [5]
                                                           66–75   [6]
                                                           76–85   [7]
                                                          over 85   [8]

Do you describe yourself as White [1], Black/African-American [2], Hispanic [3], Asian/ Pacific Islander [4], Native American [5], or some other ethnic group [6]?

About what is your total annual household income ? _____ dollars
    (Check one.)
    $20,000 or less   [1]
    $20,001 to $40,000   [2]
    $40,001 to $60,000   [3]
    $60,001 to $80,000   [4]
    above $80,000   [5]

That's all the questions I have. Thank you very much for your help. If you have any questions or comments regarding the survey, you should contact _____ at UCF. Would you like his telephone number again or his email address? By the way, you may get a call from one of my supervisors to check on my performance.

EMPLOYEE ATTITUDES

General Description

The Employee Attitudes dataset includes data from 977 employees of Seminole County Government (Florida). This *general employee survey* can easily be tailored to other research situations. Seminole County is one of five counties in central Florida. One of the smaller counties in terms of area, it includes a mix of very affluent neighborhoods, as well as some rural areas and poor neighborhoods. Human Resources Department staff conducted the survey and visited each county department. Staffs in each department were required to attend a meeting at which the anonymous and voluntary survey was administered; only a few employees chose not to participate in the survey. This is a general employee survey—employees are referred to in this county as "members"—and it includes employee assessments of working conditions, career development, benefits and compensation, supervisory management, customer relations, job skills and training, and satisfaction with Human Resources services. To ensure the anonymity of respondents, surveys were returned in sealed and unmarked envelopes, which were opened by an outside, independent consultant who did the analysis and prepared the final report.

Methods

Considerable care was taken to ensure that the questions were unbiased and consistent with questions typically found in employee surveys. During August 1999, Human Resources Department staff implemented the survey across departments and divisions by assembling all Seminole County Government employees, along with managers, for the purpose of completing the survey. Efforts were made to reach all members, and those unavailable on that day were advised of other opportunities to participate. To ensure the anonymity of members, participants were instructed not to write their name on their survey and to insert the survey into an unmarked white envelope. All envelopes were then delivered to the outside researcher, who opened and analyzed the responses.

A total of 977 surveys were received, or 84.4 percent of the 1,158 total full-time positions with Seminole County. Table W21.1 shows the distribution of these positions by department. A methodological issue is that Seminole County Government chose to state clearly that answering various standard demographic items was "voluntary," which reduced the number of completed responses for these items. The number of completed surveys is shown in Table W21.2. A question arises as to whether the lower response rates for demographic variables may result in any significant *response bias*. To explore this possibility, the aggregate responses of all respondents were compared with the responses of those who answered specific demographic questions. Typically, mean responses should differ by no more than ± 0.03, and no difference should be greater than ± 0.06. To illustrate the analysis, Table W21.3 shows the results of these three questions below, which were selected for their importance or relevance to this concern.

Item 1: "Seminole County is a good place to work for compared to other organizations I know or have worked for."

Item 2: "The quality of service provided to citizens is the same regardless of their race, gender, or background."

Item 3: "My supervisor deals fairly with everyone."

Looking over these data, we can conclude that analyses using the demographic variables are meaningful.

Finally, analysis of the data shows that some departments are quite small and that Seminole County Government has relatively few employees in each of the standard race classifications. For example, only 68 members, or 8.0 percent, of respondents identified themselves as African-American. Likewise, only 37, or 4.4 percent, identified themselves as being of Hispanic origin. The final report does not provide separate reporting for departments with either fewer than 20 respondents or less than a 50 percent response rate. Analyses of department by race contrast Caucasian and non-Caucasian employee perceptions in order to preserve the anonymity of minority respondents in each department.

Table W21.1 ⎯⎯〰⎯ Response Rate by Department

DEPARTMENT	Turned in	No. filled full-time positions	Percentage surveyed	Completed responses	Percentage self-identified of full-time positions
Administrative Services	57	57	100	51	89.5
Community Services	27	51	52.9	29	56.8
County Attorney	16	18	88.9	8	44.4
County Manager/BCC Offices	9	10	90	8	80.0
Environmental Services	129	140	92.1	102	72.8
Fiscal Services	21	21	100	13	61.9
Human Resources	13	13	100	7	53.8
Information Technologies	26	27	96.3	19	70.3
Judicial	18	22	81.8	13	59.1
Library and Leisure Services	132	158	83.5	104	65.8
Planning and Development	108	114	94.7	99	86.8
Public Safety	206	282	73.0	186	65.9
Public Works	212	238	89.1	189	79.4
Tourism	7	7	100	2	28.6
TOTAL	981	1158	85	830	71.7
Unknown				147	
TOTAL				977	

Table W22.2 ⎯⎯⎯⟍ᴧ⟋⎯ Results from Completed Surveys

Total number of full-time positions:	1,158
Completed responses:	977 (84.4%)
Identification of:	
Gender	865
Race	851
Hispanic origin	832
Pay band	674
Years employed with county	805
Department	830

Table W22.3 ⎯⎯⎯⟍ᴧ⟋⎯ Mean Answers to Items 1, 2, and 3

	Item 1 (mean)	Item 2 (mean)	Item 3 (mean)
ALL responses completed	3.64	4.31	3.51
Gender	3.66	4.33	3.52
Race	3.64	4.35	3.54
Hispanic origin	3.65	4.36	3.54
Pay band	3.67	4.32	3.47
Years employed	3.66	4.35	3.51
Department	3.64	4.32	3.52

Detailed Summary

The questions on this survey are consistent with most general employee surveys, which cover many of the same aspects discussed below. The survey instrument has 10 sections designed to assess different aspects of the workplace. The first section measures overall satisfaction with the county as a place to work. The second section assesses a broad range of general working conditions, such as the presence of safety hazards and the manner in which problems are discussed. The third section looks at employee relations with supervisors and management. The fourth section examines how customers are treated. The fifth section focuses on career development. The sixth section assesses cooperation and coordination among departments. The seventh section features questions on the adequacy of job skills and training. The eighth section delves into the quality of Human Resources services and interaction. The ninth section includes two questions about benefits and compensation. The tenth section asks a range of standard demographic questions.

Human Resources Department staff implemented the survey across departments and divisions by assembling all Seminole County Government employees (called "members"), along with managers, during regular work hours for the purpose of completing the survey. An effort was made to reach all members, and those who were unavailable on that day were advised of other opportunities to participate. To ensure the anonymity of members, participants were instructed not to write their name on their survey and to insert the survey into an unmarked white envelope. All envelopes were delivered to the analyst, after which they were opened and analyzed. Out of a total of 1,158 members, 977 returned a usable survey.

Note on Variables

The variables appear in the same order as on the survey instrument. The variable names are limited to eight characters, and the labels are consistent with the survey items. Variable values are indicated on the survey below. Missing values are coded as periods (.) in the dataset. Most items are on a five-point Likert scale.

Students using *SPSS Student Version* software will find additional information relevant to that software on the CD that accompanies this workbook.

Survey Instrument: Seminole County Government Employee Survey

The following questions are designed to assess and improve employee relations. Please evaluate the following statements by checking the appropriate box (mark an "X," please).

SA = Strongly Agree	DK = Don't Know	SD = Strongly Disagree
A = Agree	D = Disagree	

	SA	A	DK	D	SD

1. General Conditions

Overall, I am satisfied with my job at Seminole County......

5	4	3	2	1

Seminole County is a good place to work compared
to other organizations I know about or have worked for .....

Each individual is treated with dignity ....

The morale of Seminole County Government employees is
high..

In general, my department is better to work for than it was
two years ago ....

In general, Seminole County Government is a better place to
work for than it was two years ago......................

Most days I feel good about coming to work..............

I would proudly recommend Seminole County Government
as a good place to work...............................

The work that I do is important ....

Our organization welcomes change.....................

The County Newsletter is an effective communication tool ...

It is important for the organization to commit to learning
about cultural diversity...............................

My job is challenging and interesting ....

2. Working Conditions

Problems are discussed openly, candidly, and
constructively.......................................

In general, everyone seems to carry his or her fair share of
the workload ....

I have a lot of freedom to decide how to do my work........

	SA	A	DK	D	SD

I seldom feel stressed because of work . . . .

I seldom work late or past my scheduled quitting time . . . . . .

My physical working conditions are reasonable for my
type of work . . . .

The maintenance on the equipment I use is adequate . . . .

Safety hazards in my work area are quickly corrected . . . .

Most of my co-workers are receptive to trying new ways
of conducting business to improve productivity . . . .

My supervisor is skilled and experienced . . . .

3. Supervisory/Management Relations

I feel free to go to a "higher boss" than my immediate
supervisor to discuss any problems that are bothering me . . . .

Senior managers of the organization come through
my work area often . . . .

I have confidence and trust in my supervisor . . . .

My supervisor deals fairly with everyone—does not play
favorites . . . .

My division routinely holds meetings to keep people
informed . . . .

My immediate supervisor helps my work group do its best . . .

Feedback on performance is timely, accurate, and
constructive . . . .

My supervisor and I establish performance goals for the
upcoming year as part of my performance evaluation . . . .

I understand what is expected of me in my job . . . .

SA | A | DK | D | SD

4. Customer Relations

The quality of service provided to citizens is the same
regardless of their race, gender, or background . . . .

I feel very confident to make decisions or take action to
satisfy our customers. . . . .

The opinions of our customers are important to my
work group. . . . .

Most of my co-workers are receptive to trying new ways of
conducting business to improve service . . . .

5. Career Management and Rewards

Job opportunities are posted and accessible to me . . . .

When things go well in my job, my contributions are
recognized . . . .

The people that get promoted are among the best qualified
for the job . . . .

I actively participate and provide input into my performance
rating/review . . . .

Our organization has a good performance appraisal system in
place . . . .

I am familiar with the Merit Pay Program . . . .

I understand how my performance is evaluated . . . .

I am satisfied with the various member recognition
programs . . . .

I understand what I need to do to develop my career with
Seminole County Government . . . .

Internal promotions are encouraged here . . . .

6. Cooperation and Coordination

There is cooperation among departments to get the job
done . . . .

	SA	A	DK	D	SD

Our organization does a good job of keeping us informed about current developments affecting the organization ......

I understand the organization's vision, mission, goals and values ....

There is a good feeling of teamwork in my work group with people working well together ....

I am aware of my responsibilities and the procedures to follow in resolving a conflict ....

7. Job Skills and Training

Members are given challenging work that provides opportunities to learn new skills ....

Members have the skills to do their work well..............

My performance has improved as a result of attending training programs ....

I receive ongoing training to keep my skills current ....

8. Human Resource Department

The Human Resources staff is accessible and easy to work with..

The Human Resources Department does a good job of representing all employees and acting as a member advocate ....

I am comfortable seeking information and advice from Human Resources ....

I understand how the Employee Assistance Program works and its benefit to me ....

I can use the grievance procedures without fear of retribution

Our Personnel Policies Manual is well-organized and easy to work with..

SA	A	DK	D	SD

9. Benefits and Compensation

Seminole County's insurance package (health, life, and
optional coverage) meets the needs of employees . . . .

I am paid as well as people in other organizations with similar
jobs . . . .

10. Demographic Questions
Finally, the following questions are asked for the purpose of analysis, only.
Please check the appropriate boxes:

1. What is your gender?

Male	0
Female	1

2. What is your race?

Caucasian	1
African-American	2
Asian or Pacific	3
Native American	4
Other	5

3. Are you of Hispanic origin?

Yes	1
No	2

4. What is your department?

Administrative Services	1
Community Services	2
County Attorney's Office	3
County Manager/BCC	4
Environmental Services	5
Fiscal Services	6
Human Resources	7
Information Technologies	8
Judicial	9
Library & Leisure Services	10
Planning & Development	11
Public Safety	12
Public Works	13
Tourism	14

5. What is your pay band?

Pay Band 1 or 2	1
Pay Band 3 or 4	2
Pay Band 5 or 6	3
Pay Band 7, 8, or 9	4

6. How long have your worked for
Seminole County Government?

Less than 1 year	1
1+ to 3 years	2
3+ to 5 years	3
5+ to 10 years	4
10+ years	5

COMMUNITY INDICATORS

General Description

The Community Indicators dataset is developed from secondary data sources to provide a profile of cities across the United States. The 98 selected cities include many of the country's largest, as well as those from different states and a few located in rural settings. The data reflect different aspects of interest: demographic, educational, crime, environmental, transportation, sports, economic, and other concerns.

A challenge in gathering this information is that although some data are available at the city level, other data are available only at the county level, and the county boundaries do not always conform to the city boundaries. This is especially the case when data are collected not by the U.S. Census, but by other agencies. When data are collected by the U.S. Census, city estimates are available for demographic, social, educational, and housing data. We identify instances in which data were collected at the county level; many crime and health data are of this nature. In addition, we estimate, based on a visual analysis comparing maps, how well county boundaries match those of the city jurisdictions. In some cases, the fit is quite close, and in other instances it is not.

The main data sources are the U.S. Census, factfinder.census.gov (data from 2004, as available—in a few instances, the census provides only data from the 2000 census). For crime data, see U.S. Department of Justice, Uniform Crime Reporting, www.fbi.gov/ucr/cius_04/offenses_reported/index.html (2004 data). For juvenile crime data, see ojjdp.ncjrs.org/ojstatbb/ezaucr/asp/ucr_display.asp. For health data, see U.S. Department of Health and Human Services, Office on Women's Health, www.healthstatus2010.com/owh/selec_variables.aspx (data for men and women are included). Air quality data are from U.S. Environmental Protection Agency, www.epa.gov/air/data/geosel.html. For quality-of-life data, see U.S. Census Bureau, 2002 Economic Census, www.census.gov/econ/census02/guide/02EC_US.HTM.

Summary of Variables

Each variable name appears after its label.

City name—City. This is the city name, as used by the Census.

Caucasian population—Caucasian. The percent of the population that is white.

Number of persons under 18 years—UnderAge18. The number of persons in the city under age 18 years.

Number of persons from 18 through 44—Age18to44. The number of persons in the city with ages 18 through 44 years.

Number of persons from 45 through 64—Age45to64. The number of persons in the city with ages 45 through 64 years.

Number of persons over 65 years—OverAge65. The number of persons in the city over age 65 years.

Total population—Pop. Total population (estimated).

Percent of persons with high school degrees or more—HSGradorHigher. Percent of population, over age 25 years, who have a high school degree or higher degrees.

Percent of persons with bachelors degrees or more—BGradorHigher. Percent of population, over age 25 years, who have a bachelor's degree or higher degrees.

Number of violent crimes—ViolentCrime. The total number of violent crimes. According to Uniform Crime Reporting, violent crimes involve force or threat. There are four types of violent crimes: murder and non-negligent manslaughter, forcible rape, robbery, and aggravated assault. In terms of the rate of offenses for each of the four violent crimes, aggravated assault had the highest rate, estimated at 291.1 offenses per 100,000 inhabitants. There were an estimated 136.7 robberies, 32.2 forcible rapes, and 5.5 murders for each 100,000 resident population in 2004.

Murder and non-negligent manslaughter—Murder. Number of murders and non-negligent manslaughters.

Forcible rape—Rape. Number of forcible rapes.

Burglary—Burglary. Number of burglaries.

Motor vehicle thefts—MotorTheft. Number of motor vehicle thefts.

Full-time law enforcement employees—FTLaw. Number of full-time law enforcement employees.

Performing arts—PerfArts. Number of performing arts companies. Performing arts companies comprise establishments engaged primarily in producing live presentations involving the performances of actors and actresses, singers, dancers, musical groups, and other performing artists.

Museums and historical sites—MusSites. Number of museums or historic sites. Museums are described as establishments engaged primarily in the preservation and exhibition of objects of historical, cultural, and/or educational value. Historical sites are establishments engaged primarily in the preservation and exhibition of sites, buildings, forts, or communities that describe events or persons of particular historical interest.

Spectator sports—Sports. Number of spectator sport teams. Comprises sports teams or clubs participating primarily in live sporting events before a paying audience.

Unemployment rate—Unempl. Unemployment rate (includes some county-level observations).

Household income—Income. Median household income in dollars.

Rentals—Rentals. Number of households that rent.

Management and professional jobs—MgtJobs. Number of jobs in management, professional, and related occupations.

Sales and office jobs—SaleOfficeJobs. Number of jobs in sales and office occupations.

Agriculture and related jobs—AgrJobs. Number of jobs in agriculture, fishing and hunting, and mining.

Construction jobs—ConsJobs. Number of jobs in construction.

Mean travel time to work—TravelTime. Mean travel time to work (in minutes) for workers ages 16 years and older.

Use of public transportation—PublicTrans. People using public transportation for going to work, excluding taxicabs. Workers ages 16 years and older.

County-based measures:

Juvenile crime—CountyJuvCrime. Total number of juvenile crimes committed in the county. Includes violent crimes, property crimes, and nonindex crimes such as alcohol violations, forgery, fraud, and various other crimes.

Death rate—CountyDeath. Death rate in the county (2002 data).

Infant mortality rate—CountyInfant. Infant mortality rate per 100,000 population, 1996–2000.

AIDS cases—CountyAIDS. Number of AIDS cases in the county (2002 data).

Cancer cases—CountyCancer. Number of cancer cases in the county (2002 data).

Match between city and county—CityCountyMatch. Our assessment of how well the county boundaries match city boundaries. 1 = close, 2 = fair, 3 = dissimilar.

Air quality index—Air. The Air Quality Index (AQI) is an index for reporting daily air quality. The Environmental Protection Agency calculates the AQI for five major air pollutants regulated by the Clean Air Act: ground-level ozone, particle pollution (also known as particulate matter), carbon monoxide, sulfur dioxide, and nitrogen dioxide. The AQI runs from 0 to 500. The higher the AQI value, the greater the level of air pollution and the greater the health concern.

Air quality data source—AirSource. Some data are from cities; others are from counties. This variable shows the source of the AQI data only. 1 = MSA (metropolitan statistical area), 2 = county.

Counties—Counties. Counties included in the county-based measures.

WATERSHED

General Description

The Watershed dataset was developed from rating variables, explanations, descriptions, and specific data incorporated within the Environmental Protection Agency's (EPA's) Index of Watershed Indicators (IWI) website (www.epa.gov/iwi). The IWI is a compilation score determined by combining the impact of 16 measured variables used as indicators of general watershed conditions for more than 2,262 watersheds within the United States and Puerto Rico. These indicators measure the general condition of the nation's rivers, streams, wetlands, and estuaries.

Background

The 16 variables contained within the IWI are divided into two groups. The first seven variables collectively are termed *condition indicators,* and taken together they represent existing conditions of the specific watershed. (Below are the variable labels. The actual variable names appear later.) These seven condition indicators consist of "designated use attainment," "fish and wildlife consumption advisories," "drinking water impairment," "sediment contamination," "ambient water quality for four toxic pollutants," "ambient water quality for four conventional pollutants," and a "wetlands loss index" developed from two separate wetlands loss inventories. The remaining nine variables comprise the *vulnerability indicators,* which evaluate the potential for future degradation of a particular watershed. These vulnerability indicators are "aquatic/wetlands species at risk," "toxic pollutant loads discharged exceeding aggregate state permit allowance," "conventional pollutant loads discharged exceeding aggregate state permit allowance," "urban runoff potential," "index of agricultural runoff potential," "population change within the watershed," "hydrologic modifications to the watershed," "estuarine pollution susceptibility index," and an "atmospheric deposition factor." Condition indicators and vulnerability indicators are combined, yielding an IWI rating for the specific watershed.

This dataset contains four additional variables. They are the "overall watershed characteristic score," "geographical region," "population of the watershed as of the 1990 national census," and a variable describing the "wetlands loss index."

The 122 watershed observations comprising this dataset consist of two select groups of observations. First, 96 watersheds throughout the United States were specifically identified by the National Sediment Inventory as containing "Areas of Probable Concern" (www.epa.gov/OST/Events/sedlist.html). Second, an additional 26 watershed observations—chosen from sparsely populated, remote areas throughout the United States—were selected to provide comparison data for the 96 observations noted as Areas of Probable Concern. They were verified to be nonduplicative, meaning that no watershed is listed twice within the dataset. It bears comment that finding watersheds in the continental United States without some indicated degree of impairment, or expressed concern relating to their overall rating, is a difficult task.

According to the EPA, the IWI shows that 15 percent of our watersheds nationally have relatively good water quality, 36 percent have moderate problems, 22 percent have more serious water quality problems, and

27 percent cannot be characterized because of lack of information. Nationally, 1 in 15 is also highly vulnerable to further degradation.

Variable summaries provided below are intended to convey a practical understanding of the nature of each variable and why it constitutes a parameter of concern with regard to overall watershed conditions. The data collection processes inherent in the development of the IWI database involved coordination and cooperation between federal, state, tribal, and private organizations. The indicators are based on existing, published data sources collected as part of monitoring state water resources. The EPA compiles existing information on the quantity, chemical and physical composition, and geographic location of indicators shown below. Complete information addressing the collection of raw data, selection and development of variables, access to the data collection procedures and sources, and an evaluation of threshold criteria is available through the EPA IWI website.

Summary of Individual Variables: Condition Indicators

Each variable name appears after its label.

Watershed characteristic—Wshedch. This overall evaluation describes the condition of aquatic resources for a specific watershed.

Designated use attainment—Useatnmn. This variable is the percentage of water sources within a specific watershed evaluated as meeting the requirements and conditions to fully support the water source's designated uses.

Fish and wildlife consumption advisories—Advisory. When excessive levels of toxic substances are identified within watershed species, states may issue advisories warning against using specific species as a food source. These advisories may be targeted at specific population groups such as the elderly, small children, or pregnant women. This variable is the number of advisories issued within the watershed advising against the consumption of fish or aquatic wildlife. This variable is considered to be a good indicator of the general condition of a watershed and of the extent of toxic substance buildup within a watershed food chain.

Drinking water impairment—Wtrimprd. This variable provides a partial indicator of the condition of water sources within the watershed that could potentially constitute a source of drinking water. These potential sources include both ground and surface water sources sampled prior to treatment or purification for use as drinking water.

Contaminated sediments—Sedicont. This variable is a measure of the potential risks to human health and the environment determined through chemical analysis of bottom sediments, sediment toxicity data, and fish tissue residue data.

Ambient water quality (toxic pollutants)—Toxicon. This variable measures the presence and amount of copper, chromium (hexavalent), nickel, and zinc within watershed water sources. This database continues to the next data layer that provides an actual percentage of samples taken exceeding allowed levels.

Ambient water quality (conventional pollutants)—Conpolut. This variable measures the presence and amount of ammonia, dissolved oxygen, phosphorus, and pH within watershed water sources. This database continues to the next data layer providing an actual percentage of samples taken exceeding allowed levels.

Wetland loss index—Wtlds92 and Wtlnlos2. By combining two indicators, this variable measures the amount of cumulative and continuing wetlands lost. The National Resources Inventory indicates the percentage of watershed wetlands lost during the period of 1982 to 1992, while the National Wetlands Inventory estimates the percentage of watershed wetlands lost from the 1780s to the 1980s. While these two measures are combined to a single index for use within the IWI, this database continues to the next data layer and splits them back out to individual measures, Wtlds92, and Wtlnlos2, respectively. The two individual measures provide a better indication of the extent of historical wetlands loss.

Summary of Individual Variables: Vulnerability Indicators

Aquatic/wetlands species at risk—Speatrsk. This indicator represents the number of species documented in a watershed that are classified by the Heritage Network as being critically imperiled and assesses the conservation of plant and animal species at the greatest risk of extinction within the watershed.

Pollution loads discharged beyond permit limits (toxic)—Toxkdisc. Within the IWI database, this variable is listed as an aggregate index by individual state. If the total toxic pollutant discharges within the state did not exceed the total amount allowed by all permits cumulatively, then the watershed was not considered at risk. This database continues to the next data layer and documents the actual number of incidents in which individual permit discharge limits have been exceeded.

Pollution loads discharged beyond permit levels (conventional)—Convdisc. Within the IWI database, this variable is listed as an aggregate index by individual state. If the total conventional pollutant discharges within the state did not exceed the total amount allowed by all permits cumulatively, then the watershed was not considered at risk. This database continues to the next data layer and documents the actual number of incidents in which individual permit discharge limits have been exceeded.

Urban runoff potential—Urbnrnof. This variable is an indicator of the percentage of a watershed consisting of impervious surfaces (roads, paved parking lots, roofs, and so on). As the amount of impervious surfaces within a watershed increases as a result of development, natural flow patterns and volumes within streams and rivers can be altered significantly, leading to an increased potential for flooding and an increased potential for runoff of pollutants such as fertilizers and insecticides, in turn leading to further degradation of water sources within the watershed.

Agricultural runoff potential—Agrirnof. Nitrogen runoff potential from fertilizers, pesticide runoff, and sediment delivery to streams and rivers are combined in this index variable. The value for a particular watershed is ranked among 2,110 watersheds evaluated for this variable.

Population change—Popuincr. Comparison of national census data from 1980 and 1990 determined the percentage of population increase within a watershed. Increasing populations place additional burdens on watershed environments through the impact of continued development, increased exploitation of available water sources, further loss of wetlands, increased sewage flow, and additional impervious surfaces.

Hydrological modifications—Hydromod. This index is a measure of the relative amount of reservoir impoundment volume within a watershed. Dams alter natural river and stream flow rates and, when built, can lead to the loss of wetlands. Also, as water accumulates behind the dam, the resulting lake or impoundment can serve as a repository for runoff pollutant introduction, concentration, and subsequent sediment contaminant buildup.

Estuarine pollution susceptibility—Polusucp. Measuring an estuary's susceptibility to contaminant introduction and pollution buildup, this indicator is defined as an estuary's relative vulnerability to concentrations of dissolved and particulate substances. Coastal lands continue to be developed as population densities continue to shift to these regions. It should be noted that a value of "4" for this variable indicates no estuary present within the watershed for evaluation.

Atmospheric deposition—Atmosdep. Nitrogen is a primary nutrient that can cause algae blooms and other problems within watershed water sources. Atmospheric deposition primarily through precipitation is a significant source of nitrogen to these water sources. The units are kilograms per hectare per year. (One kilogram equals approximately 2.2 pounds; one hectare is 100 by 100 meters square, and approximately equal to 2.47 acres.)

Watershed population—Wtrshpop. These are the population figures as of the 1990 census.

Geographical region—Region. This is the location of the watershed within the continental United States:

> *Northeast:* Maine, Massachusetts, New Jersey, New York, Rhode Island

> *Southeast:* Alabama, Florida, Georgia, Kentucky, Louisiana, Mississippi, North Carolina, South Carolina, Tennessee

> *Midwest:* Illinois, Indiana, Kansas, Michigan, Minnesota, Missouri, Ohio, Wisconsin

> *Northwest:* Idaho, Montana, North Dakota, Oregon, South Dakota, Utah, Washington

> *Southwest:* California, Texas

> *Methodological Note:* Classified as "Northeast" are one watershed at the joint boundaries of Pennsylvania, Maryland, and West Virginia; one watershed at the joint boundaries of New York, Ohio, and Pennsylvania; and one watershed at the joint boundaries of Ohio, Pennsylvania, and West Virginia. Classified as "Southeast" is one watershed at the joint boundaries of Arkansas, Kentucky, Mississippi, Missouri, and Tennessee.

PRODUCTIVITY

General Description

This dataset contains hypothetical data about a government organization. It was created to illustrate interrelationships between employee perceptions of their work; organizational environment; and work-center, departmental, and overall organization productivity. Such data are usually obtained through employee surveys and internal administrative reports of departmental productivity.

Background

Biltrite Shipbuilding and Marine Repair is a small government shipbuilding and marine vessel repair facility located in Charleston, South Carolina. The organizational workforce is comprised primarily of federal General Schedule (GS) and Wage Grade (WG) employees. During the 1980s, Biltrite specialized in the manufacture of small coastal patrol and riverine vessels for the United States Army and the United States Coast Guard. During the 1990s the organization was involved primarily with repair of existing craft, with virtually no new construction contracts.

While Biltrite was able to remain economically viable during this period, the organization was subjected to a series of Reduction in Force (RIF) personnel actions. These RIFs resulted in a 31 percent personnel cutback over seven years. Biltrite accomplished the required cutbacks through normal employee attrition, normal retirement, and early retirement incentives. After an extended period of government defense-spending cutbacks and facilities closures, Biltrite Shipbuilding and Marine Repair now anticipates a resurgence of government military building contracts. To ensure that Biltrite is positioned as competitively as possible, the company reviewed its past productivity evaluations and compared them with those of its competition. While Biltrite's productivity does not lag behind industry averages, Biltrite does not stand out as an industry leader.

Biltrite is now evaluating alternative productivity improvement strategies, which will enhance its opportunities of being awarded future government contracts. As part of this effort, Biltrite contracted with Deeterman & Associates, a recognized leader in productivity studies within the industry. Deeterman evaluated all 10 Biltrite work centers with its four departments (see Figure W21.1).

Deeterman personnel performed the overall organizational study over a period of two months. Individual employee interviews were performed during a two-week period. All 321 Biltrite employees below the senior management level were interviewed. The survey instrument utilized was designed to assess multiple contributing aspects of three index variables and three single concept variables. Additionally, data were collected on length of employment with Biltrite and number of workdays missed because of illness over the past 12 months.

Figure W21.1 ──────᠁ᴡᴠ᠁── Biltrite Organizational Structure

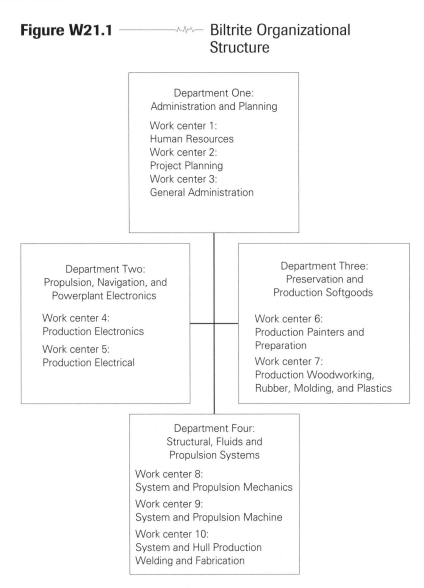

Summary of Variables

To measure the different aspects of employee satisfaction, Deeterman personnel used a seven-point Likert scale, ranging from "Strongly Disagree" to "Strongly Agree." Index variables were formed by averaging the responses to items with strong item-to-total and inter-item correlations. All variables were rescaled on a 10-point scale in which 1 = low and 10 = high.

The 12 variables studied here are listed by variable name and include the variable type and the corresponding statements from the survey.

Jobknowl. Single variable. Type: continuous. The statement evaluated by the respondent: "I have adequate skills and knowledge to perform my job."

Wkrtrtmt. Single variable. Type: continuous. The statement evaluated by the respondent: "At Biltrite, I am treated fairly and with respect."

Teamwork. An index variable (Cronbach alpha = 0.81). Type: continuous. The statements evaluated by the respondents were: "In my work center, teams are used effectively to accomplish job assignments." "I am satisfied with the functioning of my work team." "People from different work centers work well together to accomplish job assignments." "People from different departments work well together to accomplish job assignments."

Jobauthr. Single variable. Type: continuous. The statement evaluated by the respondent: "I have adequate decision-making authority to do my job well."

Recogawd. An index variable (Cronbach alpha = 0.74). Type: continuous. The statements evaluated by the respondents were: "On a day-to-day basis I understand what is expected of me by my supervisors." "In my work center, supervisors' expectations of worker performance are fair." "In my department, employee recognition and performance cash incentives are awarded fairly." "People in other departments don't have to work as hard as I do to receive the same recognition or performance cash awards." "Work done excellently is recognized at Biltrite."

Wrkdyssk. Number of workdays missed because of illness during the past 12 months. Type: continuous.

Inthempl. Length of time as Biltrite employee. Type: continuous.

Workcntr. Employee's work center. Type: categorical.

Productivity. An index variable (Cronbach alpha = 0.78). Type: continuous. The statements evaluated by the respondents were: "In my work center, employees are motivated to work." "The productivity of my work center is high." "Work activities are well planned." "My supervisor is always available to help keep projects on track." "We are always customer oriented."

Wkctrpro. Work-center productivity determined by Deeterman & Associates by examining past work-center performance data, including production planning, material procurement, availability of needed material, materials expended, man-hours scheduled and expended per production task, total and job-specific overtime man-hours expended, and percentage of production tasks requiring rework. These values were then weighted and compared with industry standards. Type: continuous.

Dprtment. The department employee's work center is located within. Type: categorical.

Deptprod. Department productivity determined by Deeterman & Associates. Type: continuous.

CRIME

General Description

This time series dataset includes data from a fictional upper midwestern U.S. metropolitan area, with a population of approximately 1 million residents. It was created to approximate the juvenile crime rate and trends in that rate, as documented by the Office of Juvenile Justice and Delinquency Prevention (OJJDP) from 1990 to 1998 (*OJJDP Statistical Briefing Book,* which can be found online at ojjdp.ncjrs.org/ojstatbb/qa260.html).

The metropolitan area known as Normalton is representative of national population demographic averages. The juvenile population is estimated by applying age distributions obtained from the *Statistical Abstract of the United States, 1998,* 118th edition. Juvenile arrest data contained within this dataset represent the average number of juvenile criminal arrests per 100,000 juveniles. Juveniles are defined as being male or female, 10 to 17 years of age.

Arrests for juvenile curfew violations are not contained within the juvenile criminal arrest variables. Rather, they are represented within the specific curfew violation arrest variable Curfviol.

Unemployment figures averaged over the year represent national rates obtained from the Bureau of Labor Statistics. A variation was inserted to represent the hiring practices associated with areas that evidence a seasonal tourist economic component.

Background

In June 1993 the city council of Normalton and the newly elected mayor, the Honorable I. M. Worthyman, received from the chief of police the annual report on Normalton crime. The report indicated that, as in the rest of the nation, juvenile crime in Normalton had continued to rise. This report lent further support to an identified upward trend in juvenile crime that began in 1989.

In July 1993 an Australian family was violently attacked and robbed outside their Normalton hotel by a gang of youths. Their daughter was paralyzed as a result of the injuries received during the attack. This family represented only 5 of the typical 1.2 million tourists drawn to Normalton each spring, summer, and fall by its widely heralded natural beauty, ecological diversity, and three world-class roller coaster theme parks. The case drew national attention.

Feeling that the city must take action to halt what was perceived as an upwardly spiraling juvenile crime rate, the mayor and city council proposed a strict juvenile curfew. Following a survey of city residents, which indicated broad support for the initiative, the city council drafted and unanimously passed a juvenile curfew to take effect on January 1, 1994. The curfew affected all juveniles between the ages of 10 and 17, requiring them to be off the streets between the hours of 8 p.m. and 1 a.m., unless they were in transit to or from an official recreational event or a church function, or were accompanied by an adult. All juveniles were required to be at home after 1 a.m.

The city council also passed a parental responsibility law, whereby parents found negligent in exercising proper control and supervision of their children could be held legally responsible for their children's legal transgressions, including curfew violations. This law took effect on March 1, 1994.

By 1999 there were questions about the effectiveness of the curfew, as the mayor was preparing to run for another term.

Summary of Variables

The listing below shows the variable names, a brief definition of each of the variables, and the variable type. The dataset also includes the first-order differences of these variables, shown as Crimar_1, Juvars_1, Curfi_1, Parenr_1, Curfew_1, Juvnco_1, and Unempl_1.

Crimarst. Number of total juvenile criminal arrests by month from January 1, 1990, through December 31, 1998. Type: continuous.

Juvarsts. Number of monthly juvenile criminal arrests between 8 p.m. and 1 a.m., January 1, 1990, through December 31, 1998. Type: continuous.

Curfviol. Total juvenile arrests for curfew violations, by month. Type: continuous.

Policcur. Number of police per shift dedicated to juvenile code enforcement. Type: continuous.

Month. Month of year. Type: categorical.

Month. A dummy variable of each month. For example, Month1 denotes January, Month2 denotes February, and so forth. Type: categorical.

Befraftr. Number of daily juvenile criminal arrests between 8 p.m. and 1 a.m. 54 days before and 54 days after implementing juvenile curfew restrictions. Type: continuous.

Parenrsp. Number of parents held legally responsible for their children's violations. Type: continuous.

Unemploy. Percentage of Normalton labor force unemployed. Type: continuous.

Juvncort. Juvenile criminal cases adjudicated in juvenile court. Type: continuous.

TIME

General Description

All the variables in the Time dataset are hypothetical. The dataset was developed to illustrate problems relating to simple and multiple regression, as discussed in Chapters 15 and 17 of the textbook. The Time dataset is used for exercises in Chapters 15 and 17 of this workbook. Specifically, these exercises deal with the following problems:

1. Identifying and removing outliers
2. Performing regression with dummy variables
3. Nonlinear relations among variables
4. Autocorrelation

Each problem is associated with a different exercise, and the variables associated with each exercise are defined in the next section.

Summary of Variables

The dataset contains four different sets of variables:

1. **Two variables, Fishcon and Contam1, represent measurements taken from different parts of a large lake in order to test the hypothesis that alleged water pollution is affecting the stock of certain fish.**
    Fishcon = The concentration of fish.
    Contam1 = The concentration of a water pollutant.

2. **The Time dataset also contains observations from 35 hypothetical cities regarding the use of citizen focus groups in various departments (Focus). The data are based on a survey. Most variables are index variables taken from different survey questions. The variables are defined as follows:**

    Focus = A composite measure of the breadth and depth of the use of citizen focus groups in a city. Varies from 0 (low) to 20 (high).
    Mgrint = A measure of the city manager's interest in obtaining citizen-based feedback. Varies from 1 (low) to 4 (high).
    Pubcompl = A measure of public complaints about the quality and effectiveness of a wide range of municipal services. Varies from 1 (low) to 8 (high).
    Budget = Indicates whether municipal budgets have increased in the past two years. Values: −1 = decrease in budget; 0 = no change in budget; 1 = increase in budget. Size = City size. Varies from 1 = small to 7 = large.
    Region = An indicator variable of the region in which the city is located.
    Values: 1 = Northeast; 2 = South; 3 = Midwest; 4 = West.

3. **It is commonly hypothesized that crimes are more frequent in large cities. The dataset contains the following variables:**

    Nvcrime = Index of nonviolent crimes in a given year.
    Citysize = City size.

4. **Time series data are common in program evaluation and public policy. These variables examine the impact of a law, which, among other things, increases jail time for driving under the influence (DUI). The dataset contains the following variables:**

    Fatal = Traffic fatalities per 100,000 miles driven.
    Year = Year of traffic fatalities measured.
    Short = A dummy variable identifying when the policy intervention occurred, namely, in 1980 when a law was passed that requires mandatory jail time for DUI. Values: 0 = pre-law adoption (pre-1980), and 1 = post-law adoption (post-1980).
    Long = A dummy variable identifying the number of years of post-policy adoption. Values: 0 = for pre-law adoption, 1 = for 1980, 2 = for 1981, 3 = for 1982, and so forth. This variable gives weight to long-term effects of policy.
    Jailtime = Days of jail time served by offenders because of the law.